Disability Voice
Towards an Enabling Education

Mal Leicester

Jessica Kingsley Publishers
London and Philadelphia

The right of Mal Leicester to be identified as author of this work has been asserted by him in accordance with the Copyright, Designs and Patents Act 1988.

First published in the United Kingdom in 1999 by
Jessica Kingsley Publishers Ltd
116 Pentonville Road
London N1 9JB, England
and
325 Chestnut Street
Philadelphia, PA 19106, U S A

Copyright © Mal Leicester 1999

www.jkp.com

Library of Congress Cataloging in Publication Data
A CIP catalogue record for this book is available from the Library of Congress

British Library Cataloguing in Publication Data
Leicester, Mal
Disability voice: towards an enabling education
1. Special education 2. Mainstreaming in education
I. Title
371.9'1

ISBN 1 85302 355 8

Printed and Bound in Great Britain by
Athenaeum Press, Gateshead, Tyne and Wear

341872

Contents

Acknowledgements

I would like to thank Denise Mottershead and Diane Layton for typing my manuscript and record my considerable gratitude to Felicity Fletcher-Cambell, Jack Cohen and Ann Lewis, all of whom gave me extremely useful comments on an earlier draft of this book. I am also deeply indebted to my brother, Edward Leicester, who helped me to organise my material and to Tessa Lovell, who worked with me on the 'Disability Voice' project. Finally, my warm thanks to all the people who gave generously of their time in interviews and who were willing to share their experiences.

CHAPTER I

The Voice of Experience

Introduction

This book is concerned with equal opportunities for disabled people, particularly in and through education, and approaches this issue in a new way. Most writing about the experience of disabled people consists of an author's views and, sometimes, that writer's personal experience or research. This book, however, is based on, and incorporates, the words of disabled people themselves. Thematically structured to highlight significant patterns in the collective experience of many individuals, Chapters 2, 3 and 4 provide a channel for this voice of experience – the experience of the disabled and of parents of disabled children, particularly in relation to education.

My own experience as the parent of a 'severely disabled' daughter (see page 11) motivated my writing the book and was a significant factor in the decision to approach the issue of education through the direct experience of disabled people.

Following the Warnock Report (1978) there has been more focus on the issue of integrating disabled children into mainstream schools. With the controversial 'care in the community' policy of the previous Conservative government there has also been a greater focus on community-based living for disabled adults and on the needs of carers. Moreover, the disability rights movement has strengthened and pushed forward civil rights legislation and we have the Disability Discrimination Act 1995. The advocacy movement is concerned to protect the rights of individuals in vulnerable groups who may lack some skills to protect their own interests – people with learning difficulties, for example. All this has added to a greater recognition that contemporary concern to develop equal opportunities in education is important for disabled people, just as it is for women and members of minority ethnic groups. However, these cautiously progressive contemporary developments have taken place in a society in which the endemic prejudice and wide-scale discrimination against people with disabilities (Swain 1993) in education, as in the wider society, continues to damage seriously the quality of people's lives and is severely disempowering. The aim of what follows, then, is to provide a forum for the expression of this shared experience of discrimination, particularly in relation to education, and to explore the implications of it for the development of a more adequate and enabling lifelong education.

I hope that the book will be of interest to disabled people and their families, and that it will also be read by educational policy makers and educators. It is important that policy and practice in the provision of educational services, both for people with disabilities and in terms of a disability-aware education for all, be informed by an understanding of significant aspects of the educational experiences, needs and opinions of disabled people. Such an understanding should influence practical decisions in education towards increased good practice. Similarly, greater disability awareness in the construction of academic knowledge about institutional discrimination would increase our theoretical understanding, and I hope that academics in education and other social sciences will assimilate the voice of experience reflected in the chapters to come.

Terminology

Widespread social prejudice and stereotyping are often expressed in verbal harassment through derogatory terms and labels (e.g. racial prejudice: 'wog'; gender prejudice: 'bitch'; age prejudice: 'old trout'; disability prejudice: 'cripple', 'dummy'). The majority of people do not use such intentionally abusive terms, though, sadly, many of our respondents had been subjected to this kind of abuse. However, widespread negative attitudes tend to affect us all and to find expression in our language in more subtly offensive terms and assumptions (e.g. 'coloured' people; 'he' as a generic term for all people; 'old age pensioner'; 'physically (or mentally) handicapped' person). Of course, education aims to confront and change prejudiced attitudes and not just our language at a superficial level. However, some sensitivity to terminology can both reflect and encourage attitudinal change as well as simultaneously encouraging language which is less hurtful to individuals in socially disfavoured groups.

It is a good general principle to use the terms preferred by members of those groups themselves. Preferred terms change over time because of the connection between language and attitudes. Currently, 'disabled people' is used by, for example, many writers who are part of a civil rights movement and by self-advocacy groups. They have pointed out that if they have to be referred to *en masse*, 'disabled people' should mean ordinary people who are disabled by social barriers and disabling institutions. It is the term used, therefore, in that sense, in this book. It refers to people with social disability as a consequence of physical or learning impairments.

'Impairment' is a descriptive term for the loss of a function (e.g. sight) and may disable the impaired person (e.g. being unable to read print). People are not less valuable because they have an impairment not shared by a majority of people. 'Handicap', however, occurs when those who are impaired are discriminated against (e.g. by an environment that fails to provide books in Braille or by patronising attitudes from the sighted). Thus handicap is not an attribute of an individual but a condition arising from an interaction with an inadequate social world.

There has been much discussion of the terms 'integration' and 'inclusion'. Briefly, 'integration' has been used (as in the Warnock Report) to imply moving children who are formally segregated in special schools into mainstream schools to learn alongside their non-disabled peers. Integration is not necessarily a once-only event, but more sensibly a staged process from partial to full mainstream inclusion. Integration need not be an 'all or nothing' matter either, since some children may benefit from part of their education taking place in a special school or unit and part in the mainstream. The term 'integration' is sometimes used narrowly, without the recognitions just mentioned. The term 'inclusion' incorporates these more enlightened ideas about the process and conditions by which a disabled person is part of the mainstream. Indeed, it tends to reflect an awareness that with a more enlightened perspective on disability, the aim is not to bring a disabled child into an unchanged mainstream school, but to achieve a mainstream provision which caters for all children, with their range of abilities, disabilities and needs. The connotation of the term, then, is one of the acceptance of student diversity. In this book, because our respondents tended to use the term 'integration', its use has been retained, though I have used 'inclusion' where I want to emphasise the more enlightened perspective.

Negative perspectives and assumptions about disabled people often derive from the notion that they deviate from a norm – are not 'normal'. It is strange that we should overvalue sameness and conformity. It seems to me that, within moral and legal boundaries, it is both more humane and more intelligent to value diversity of talents, interests, pursuits, ways of life, values, appearances and so on.

Many of our respondents felt that disabled people are labelled and devalued. They are labelled in this sense: once they are placed in the category of 'disabled person' this becomes the whole story – 'their' disability is always taken to be the most significant fact about them even though in most situations it is an irrelevant one.

It is a deeply educative and lifelong task to become increasingly aware of the assumptions and values built into our ways of thinking, speaking and behaving. These interact in that prejudiced thinking encourages discriminatory words and deeds which tend to escalate (Allport 1958). Fortunately, one may learn to become more critical of unwarranted assumptions, beliefs and values about whole groups of people, and disability and racism awareness training and so on address this educative task directly and explicitly. Without such critical awareness we are more likely to see and devalue individuals through the distorting blinkers of social stereotypes and thus, even with good intentions, to act, think and speak in a discriminatory and harmful manner.

Disability Voice

From 1990–92 Tessa Lovell, my research associate, and I investigated equal opportunity practice in British universities. We explored, using a triangulation of questionnaires, telephone interviews and visits, the practices of a range of departments in each institution and sought to identify good practice in relation to ethnicity, gender and special needs. One of our findings was that there is a relative lack of a social perspective on disability (a perspective explored below) and, correspondingly, little disability awareness in departmental practice or provision – both in relation to the education of all students and also in connection with catering for special needs (Leicester and Lovell 1992). During this period Tessa Lovell, an active and energetic young woman, was diagnosed as having multiple sclerosis and I, an older academic, had brought up a 'severely disabled' daughter who had been educated in special schools and, now in her 20s, was still living at home and having negative experiences of post-school training and the search for employment. The combination, for both of us, of considerable professional experience in the field of equal opportunities and education, and personal experiences in connection with impairment, led to our decision to explore the educational experience of people with disabilities.

During 1993–95 Tessa Lovell interviewed 18 adults with impairment and I interviewed 10 parents of disabled children. They were lightly structured but probing interviews and our own personal experiences generated a good rapport, which seemed to encourage our interviewees to be very open with us. The methodological question of how far such shared experience is necessary for the attainment of good data is complex and interesting and not in any way 'settled' by our 'subjective' assessment on the basis of our limited experience. It is worth noting, however, that at least one-third of our respondents told us, spontaneously, that they found it easy to talk to us because 'you understand', because 'you've been through this too'.

It might be asked why, though we interviewed disabled adults and the parents of disabled children, we did not interview any children – particularly disabled children. It was partly because we believed that by interviewing individuals with whom we shared relevant experiences (Tessa with disabled adults and myself with parents of disabled children) our empathy would encourage richer interview responses. (Certainly our data are extensive and enlightening.) Moreover, we knew that a colleague at Warwick University was interviewing children to probe their attitudes to disability. I recommend her book about this (Lewis 1995) and, where appropriate to a particular theme, particularly link schemes in connection with 'inclusion', I have incorporated, in summary, some of her findings.

Lewis concludes from her research (and consonant with the work of others) that, carefully monitored, the inclusion of disabled children in mainstream education is a feasible and reasonable goal. The achievement of this goal would benefit 'mainstream' and disabled children. She ends her book with the words of a 36-year-old man with Down's Syndrome (Lewis 1995):

> People should realise that we are people like them and want to be treated like them, so that you are in the same standards. But, not saying, 'Well I want to be your friend because you're handicapped!' To me that is wrong, totally, generally. It would be much nicer to know people coming up to say 'I'm your friend and I want to know more about you as a person', not just that big word that doesn't mean anything. (p.180)

Many of our interviewees said that they had not before had anyone outside the family to listen to their experiences and feelings, that they were pleased to share their experiences, views and reflections with us, and that they valued the experience. Some of them wept when recounting painful experiences. The research process itself was, for both researchers and interviewees, emotionally taxing but worthwhile. We were listening to accounts of suffering that resonated with our own experiences, to accounts of prejudice and discrimination that made us angry, and of courage and love which drew our admiration.

Groups were carefully selected to represent a wide range of different kinds of impairment and our sample included women and men from different class, ethnicity and age groups. We used a variety of ways of contacting individuals – courses, word of mouth, disability organisations, educational networks, a citizen advocacy project, social services – to achieve a random sample from within our selected groups. We interviewed each other to include our own experiences legitimately within our research data. The interviews were tape recorded and transcribed, and yielded rich, detailed personal biography about educational experience.

Significant patterns of shared experience emerged. In other words, many experiences were so common, so frequently repeated in or after interview (indeed, most of these shared experiences figured unanimously) that they deserve to be considered by relevant policy makers and professionals. These were clearly significant experiences, not just because of their high frequency of mention within and across interviews, but also because they were emotionally intense and had an impact on the quality of our respondents' lives. For example, all but one parent described a painful process of learning about his or her child's impairment which had been exacerbated by inadequate and insensitive communication on the part of the health professionals concerned. Many adult respondents had experienced increasingly negative social attitudes towards them as they grew into adulthood and most provided a bleak picture in relation to careers advice, and some in relation to vocational training and employment. These and other significant patterns of experience are analysed in Chapters 3 and 4 and are illuminated by the words of those who were interviewed.

Our ethical belief that policy makers and educators ought to listen to marginalised voices, and our epistemological assumption (discussed below) that intersubjective agreement in the experiences of those in marginalised groups can enrich our 'objective' educational knowledge, were endorsed by the substantive findings of the research. As we shall see, respondents did feel that their 'voice' was not being attended to and clearly there was a shared agreement about what experiences and issues were important and why. It was because of these mutually endorsing interactions of theoretical assumptions and research findings that the project came to be referred to as 'disability voice'.

Autobiography, Shared Experience and Knowledge

There is, increasingly, a recognition of the importance of personal experience in the learning process; it affects how individuals learn and can be used in adult education as a pedogogical resource. Students can learn from each other by sharing and analysing their own and others' experiences about the social world. When the focus is on personal experience of discrimination and oppression this is known as a 'radical pedagogy' through which a consciousness of the interrelation of the personal and political can be achieved, together with a much deeper understanding of oppressive social structures (see, for example, Giroux 1992).

There is also more recognition of the importance of narrative and biography in informing practice (see, for example, a special issue of the *Journal on Moral Education*). The use of 'life history' has become a tool of qualitative educational research (see, for example, a special issue of the *Journal of the British Sociological Association*). The academic claim is that a life story becomes 'life history' and thus part of our objective knowledge in the context of the stories of others and/or when supported by other evidence. Our respondents' life stories were mutually supportive and endorsed by research findings (see, for example, Derrington, Evans and Lee 1996; Lee and Henkhuzens 1996). On a practical, common-sense level, too, many educators have recognised that if educational provision is to serve the whole community, it must be especially open to the voices of less powerful and privileged social groups. Certainly the 'disability voice' research, as I have indicated, revealed a widely shared experience of 'not being heard' by professionals. A communication isolation was one of the many instances of a significant shared pattern of experience which emerged, spontaneously and almost unanimously, from the life stories of those to whom we talked. There was also some evidence of social isolation. Of course, it could be said that those who are socially isolated may be more ready to talk to a researcher. However, many of our respondents were not obviously isolated themselves (students, professional 'carers') but spontaneously commented on their isolation at some other point in their lives or about the current isolation of other disabled individuals whom they knew.

The epistemological thesis that the objectivity required by 'knowledge' can be derived from shared experience is an influential one. Wittgenstein, for example, argued that our shared agreements in primitive reaction and propensities make possible shared conceptualisation of the world and thus shared experiences of it (Wittgenstein 1953). Lacan, Foucault, Derrida and Habermas along with other influential writers also rely on constructivist epistemological assumptions in their work on meaning and communication (i.e. the idea that our shared concepts are socially constructed as distinct from simply given to us by reality as it 'really is', unaffected, as it were, by the human mind and the nature of the social world). The current postmodernist emphasis on a plurality of perspectives encourages the idea that there may be some differences in the conceptual constructions of distinct social/cultural worlds and therefore some valid differences in perspectives.

I suggest that there is a significant epistemological difference between the private experience of a single individual and experiences that have been found to be shared by many, and that this is the crucial difference between a subjective belief and objective knowledge. For example, if only one black individual claimed to have experienced negative discrimination based on ethnicity, this would be a subjective claim. It is because such experiences are widely shared by black people in Britain that we regard such claims in general (though not necessarily each and every separate alleged incident) as based on a social truth about the racist nature of our society. Different groups do sometimes have different experiences of the world and, in that sense, different but valid perspectives on it. Thus black people (in general) have more direct understandings of the many and sometimes subtle forms which racism may take. Widely shared experiences of a particular social group, then, rightly count as contributing to our collective knowledge of the social world. Our collective deafness to the experience of disabled people may be more damaging to disabled individuals than an individual's literal deafness need be.

Because the shared experiences of a group of individuals are the research basis of this study, it is important to recognise the validity of a theoretical framework which objectifies this subjective experience. Acceptance that the voice of individuals be part of our theoretical speculations is, as I have indicated, in line with current approaches to 'metaphysical' and epistemological questions. The postmodernist distrust of 'grand narrative' has given greater emphasis to smaller-scale theoretical projects, and while meta-theory may be suspect, the 'particular' gains validity, and the emphasis on plurality of perspective endorses the significance of marginalised voices.

At a less abstract level, there has always been recognition (in fiction, for example) that we can explore general issues through particular narratives. The merely anecdotal becomes significant when it resonates interpersonally. The experiences drawn upon in the following chapters have that kind of resonance.

Patterns of Experience

Although our chief concern is with education, because this takes place within a wider social context, Chapter 2 explores that context. How do broader social structures and provisions affect people with disabilities? Our respondents talked about how their impairment was diagnosed and communicated to them by various health professionals and about what forms of support were needed and what available, including issues about access, leisure and transport. They discussed the public and private attitudes to their disability which they had encountered and which informed their views about social attitudes to disability. They also recounted both positive and negative experiences of living and being educated in this society. These 'non-educational' issues are interesting in themselves; they do also, of course, have educational implications. These are drawn out as they arise and are returned to in Chapter 5.

Chapter 3 deals directly with schooling – the school-based educational experiences and opinions of our respondents. What were their shared and key experiences of schooling for those with 'special educational needs'? What do the parents whose children are currently in special schools have to say about special schools and about the process of statementing their child? And what do our respondents think about issues around integration?

Our emphasis on the importance of 'personal experience' can be discerned in several current movements in adult education. For example, it is central in APEL (the accreditation of prior experiential learning) (Griffin 1987), in the notion of 'the reflective practitioner' (Schön 1983), in participatory research and, as previously mentioned, in the idea of a radical pedagogy. Chapter 4 explores education beyond school. What, in general, has been the experience for disabled adults of further and higher education, of post-school careers advice and training, and of on-going learning in employment? What do disabled people have to say about mainstream continuing and lifelong education for us all?

It is in Chapters 2, 3 and 4, then, that significant patterns of experience are highlighted and illuminated by the words and experiences of disabled people. By 'patterns of experience' I mean, as I have indicated, both those experiences which occur in all, or almost all, of the responses of those interviewed and also those experiences which pattern (many) individual lives by occurring and recurring in various forms at key points throughout each life story. For example, the issue of 'aesthetic dissonance' (people reacting – either by staring or deliberately averting their gaze from any person who looks 'different') was mentioned in different contexts by several individuals, and the issue of lack of information about existing resources and support systems occurred and recurred throughout each life story. Key points in a life history were often experienced as a life crisis when timely information and support could have made a huge difference. Consider this mother of a child with Down's Syndrome commenting on her experiences after she herself was diagnosed as having muscular sclerosis:

> I just got on with it but obviously when something like that happens it does make it very difficult and it becomes very hard to get back out of that pit because it's like climbing up somewhere with straight sides. You won't reach the top because nobody is there to help you.

In Chapter 5, some conclusions are drawn and recommendations made. These recommendations concern educational policy and practice, affecting a wide range of professionals, including those in the health and welfare fields, those in special schools, those in mainstream schools, in teacher education, in adult education, in careers services, and in vocational and professional education.

Models of Disability: A Caring Justice and Judicious Care

There are different perspectives on disability. These differences in the way we conceive of and theorise about disability make a huge difference to the treatment which people with disabilities receive in all areas of social life, and to the endemic prejudices to which they are exposed. In what follows I indicate some of the major differences between perspectives – in particular the difference between 'individual' and 'social' theories. I shall indicate my own perspective, which draws upon disparate theories.

There is considerable evidence that discrimination against the disabled is widespread (see, for example, Mittler and Sinason 1996) and also that there is little general recognition of the degree to which institutional and indirect discrimination function against disabled people (see, for example, Leicester and Lovell 1994a).

This general lack of awareness hampers the move from rhetoric to real equality and integration on equal terms. As Paul Abberley (1987) and others have argued, people meet with endemic prejudice and structural discrimination which significantly restrict choice and badly affect the quality of their lives. The degree to which a disability handicaps one is conditional upon social policies and practices. Though we all have our own unique range of abilities and disabilities, the majority label a minority 'the disabled', subject them to separate provision, and respond to them with fear and distaste. In the majority of cases, the very people so labelled have paid a price for the general good, incurring impairment from the downside of modern developments and progress such as inoculations, road accidents, industrial machinery, pollution, medical drugs, the weapons of war and so on. Abberley thus argues that disability is a form of oppression – an oppression which creates a passive sub-class of welfare recipients to serve as a powerful warning against falling off the achievement ladder.

Such a perspective on disability rests on a social model of disability which underpins the developing disability movement (Hasler 1993) and which defines disability as 'socially imposed restriction'. Disability is not conceived of as a condition of the individual. The experiences of disabled people are of social restrictions in the world around them; the individual's experience of disability is created in interactions with a physical and social world designed for non-disabled living.

A distinction could be made here between 'disability' and 'impairment'. Many people would not choose to be impaired, but the degree to which their impairment restricts their lives (disables them) is largely socially conditioned.

The social model of disability contrasts with other models which locate the problems of disability firmly with the individual. For example, the medical model sees disability as an illness, and thus pathologises many fit and healthy individuals. (It is impairment, not disability, that may sometimes be medically alleviated.) And the 'personal tragedy theory' conceives of disabled people as victims of tragic happenings and circumstances. (In effect this is to conflate disability and impairment.) Social theories encourage social interaction based on notions of equal rights and social policy geared towards compensating individuals, but it is these individual-centred perspectives which currently dominate both social interactions and social policies.

There are varieties of individual and of social theories, depending on underpinning sociological theories about the relationship between individual and society, and on philosophical assumptions about the construction of knowledge. For example, a distinction has been made between 'creationist' social models and 'constructionist' social models. In 'creationist' models, disability is the material product of societal development within a particular historical context and the units of analysis are disabling barriers, physical, structural and institutional, and relations of power. In 'constructionist' models, disability is taken to be the product of societal development within a specific cultural context where the units of analysis are cultural values and representations, these being relative to a culture and leading to various kinds of social labelling and role expectations. Priestley (1998) has explicated these distinctions, pointing out that social models do not deny impairment but emphasise social aspects of our world that can be changed. They are important because they emphasise collective action against collective discrimination – particularly creationist models which concentrate attention on civil rights and the removal of barriers. Certainly, in seeking social change, this emphasis on power differentials and abuse of power is crucial. However, in our complex world it may be that being too dichotomous in our perspectives (this theory but not that) is not conducive to complete understanding and comprehensive social change. Cultural values, as well as material barriers, adversely affect the lives of materially disadvantaged groups. Moreover, for the educator, the individual learner, in his or her particular situation, is central. Thus I want to develop a perspective on disability which emphasises the creationist model of disability, but which incorporates recognition of the constructionist model and even elements of the individual model too.

Sally French has also emphasised the social model while retaining a broad sense of the complexity of disabled experience. She has argued that to establish a disability movement with some hope of improving the lives of disabled people, it is necessary that the social model of disability should become more widely shared (French 1993). Similarly, I want to suggest that to include disabled children in mainstream educational provision with some hope of their acceptance on equal terms, this social perspective on disability must become shared by mainstream teachers and pupils. (This is not to deny that other factors are also important; factors such as decently differentiated curricula and relevant pedagogical skills.)

However, French also argues that we need to broaden our understanding to reflect the complexity of the experiences of people with disabilities, and to recognise that not all the problems experienced by people with some kinds of impairment can be solved by social manipulation. (The distinction previously made between 'impairment' and 'disability' reflects this difference in 'social solvability'. Indeed, impairment cannot be solved by social manipulation, but disability often can.)

It seems to me that the experience of many disabled people encompasses emotional and physical pain, suffering and frustration associated with loss of a function(s) and the experience of socially imposed restrictions such that this impairment is more disabling than it need be.

A perspective on disability that integrates the personal and the political (the individual and the social) would indeed, as French suggests, be more true to lived experience. Certainly the 28 individuals interviewed in our research all described both experiences of suffering and experiences of encountering prejudice, discrimination and lack of adequate or appropriate provision. For example, many of the parents claimed that the facilities to meet educational needs identified in their child's statement had not been provided. But all the interviewees also talked of experiences of distress. The process of learning about their own or their child's impairment was a difficult one, and it was often compounded by inadequate empathy on the part of doctors and by lack of social support structures to offer counselling or information or practical advice.

One young woman, for example, insisting on tests against her doctor's insistence that she was suffering only from stress, learned of her multiple sclerosis like this: 'The hospital said, "well here is a note for your doctor, which is saying what is wrong with you and can you give it to your doctor?" They didn't even bother to lick it down. And they knew I would look and that was their way of telling me.'

Without a social perspective on disability, compassion and empathy degenerate into pity and the 'disabled' are marginalised and pathologised; awareness of social discrimination is obscured. But without an understanding of the individual's often physically and emotionally taxing experience of impairment, we may risk failing to empathise with the actual individuals we meet. If we integrate these perspectives we can, perhaps, on the one hand recognise the importance of justice, rights and of ending discrimination, while on the other retaining a compassionate understanding of the suffering of others, and of the diversity and uniqueness of individual experiences, circumstances and needs. Such an integrated perspective on disability emphasises both justice and care. Social, including school, policy could be anti-oppressive in relation to disability and compensatory in relation to impairment.

If we can encourage children and teachers to develop this broad perspective on disability, their attitudes and actions may be more likely to combine considerations of justice and feelings of compassion. This may enable disabled children to have happier experiences of integration on equal terms.

In the past, the values of justice and care have underpinned dichotomous moral frameworks. I think that these can also be bridged to produce a moral orientation consonant with this broad conception of disability (Leicester 1994). We need not choose to base our moral actions and decisions either on a coldly impartial justice or on a care ethic that disregards principles of fair treatment. Let us combine a caring justice with a just compassion.

A 'Seeing Justice and Judicious Care'

We can distinguish two different moral traditions: one focused on justice and one on care. John Rawls (1971), for example, is concerned with impartial, rational judgements. In order that decisions about what is in the general good are not affected by personal considerations, these judgements are made from behind a 'veil of ignorance'. Jesus of Nazareth, on the other hand, focused on love. Loving other people should guide our behaviour towards them. The difference between the influential work of Kohlberg (1981) on moral development and that of Gilligan's 'feminist' critique of it (1982) has been widely seen as embodying a justice versus care dichotomy of moral orientation.

In her article, 'Women and ethics: a seeing justice?', Hepburn (1994) argues that an inclusive moral framework, integrating Kohlberg's concern with justice in moral decision making with Gilligan's focus on care, would be more satisfactory than either alone:

> In order to acknowledge appropriately human capacities to identify with others and to appreciate a range of perspectives an integration of reason and sentiment in ethical analysis is required. Such a style of approach embodies a 'seeing' rather than a 'blind' justice because it depends upon giving attention to particularities as well as generalities. (p.?)

Justice, in this context, requires an attempt to see the issue from another's point of view and not just 'how I would see it if I were in that position'. This allows that experiences arising from different life situations and social positions influence moral perspectives – not distorting our judgements but enriching them through comprehending the perspectives of others. There is an emphasis here on context and human interrelatedness and interdependence, rather than on universalisability and individual autonomy.

Other feminist writers have also found traditional conceptions of justice too limited. Thus Friedman (1987) points out that Rawls's account may fail to uncover special duties of justice which arise in close personal relationships. She points out that motherhood tends to present its practitioners with moral problems best seen in terms of a complex framework which integrates justice with care, since the needs of the weaker family members often have to take precedence over the interests of the stronger. Millet (1987) also observes that moral commitments always take place in the context of specific relations with others. Baier (1987) suggests that the prizing of individual effort (rather than co-operative enterprise) allows the subordination of others to be tolerated whereas, with a 'care perspective', to fail to compensate the less independent would be construed as neglect.

Hepburn raises the question of how, then, we can integrate sentiment with reason to produce a 'seeing justice'. Her main suggestions are that we should remove the veil of ignorance and seek the views of those about whom the decisions are being made; that we should be influenced by contextual detail; and that we should make a conscious effort to apply both justice and care perspectives, sequentially, in working towards a final, integrated decision.

In the context of the concerns of this book, this means that the views of disabled people should be part of determining 'special' provision; that we should take specific, individual factors into account in providing for each particular student; and that educational decisions should be characterised by fairness to all pupils, consideration of each pupil's rights and empathetic understanding of the vulnerabilities of particular pupils.

Surely, in making educational decisions we want to achieve actions that are both just *and* caring. I agree with Hepburn that to integrate justice and care produces a better moral framework for decisions: that is both because, as she argues, blind justice (justice without care) may fail to take account of special relationships and particular needs; but also, and conversely, because an injudicious caring (care without justice) is lopsided too. Care without justice may be unfair to those who are less dependent or less in need of compassionate understanding.

In making decisions about integrating disabled children we have to bear in mind the interests of all children as well as of the disabled child. This is why, for example, some highly emotionally disturbed children may not be able to be accommodated in an ordinary school, with children whom they might harm (Samad and Fairburn 1992).

To sum up, then, we want to act in ways that are both caring and just and, therefore, to bridge both moral frameworks as we make our decisions. What I have suggested about synthesising social and personal perspectives on disability supports, and is supported by, this suggestion that we need a caring justice and judicious care. A social perspective on disability encourages justice – a recognition of universal rights and anti-oppressive policies – and can incorporate an understanding of the suffering often associated with impairment. When considerations about justice and feelings of care influence our educational decisions, we will not pursue justice at the expense of empathetic understanding of the diversity and uniqueness of individual need, nor allow our caring to become either patronising or unfair.

Education for All

Successful integration of disabled children into ordinary schools has implications for (part of) the (moral) education of all children. This is so in obvious and direct ways. For example, children will need to unlearn prejudices about those with disabilities, to question stereotypes and to value diversity. These are also familiar aspects of the attitudinal and values dimensions of antiracist, multicultural education (Leicester 1989).

We need to teach children to appreciate the views of others. They should develop the commitment and skills to 'hear' marginalised voices. They will require practice in taking account of contextual details; to learn to recognise the diversity of individual needs and to understand that 'equality of treatment' is not always equivalent to 'sameness of treatment'. They will need an understanding of the social theory of disability and the ability to empathise with the suffering often associated with impairment. More generally, one might say, they will need practice in synthesising/inclusive/contextual forms of thought (a feminist educational influence). Thus 'personal, social and moral' education will include the development of universalising and contextual thought processes. And it will connect with the education of the emotions, through the development of a loving disposition.

I find it interesting that, in thinking about values education and the integration of disabled children, both antiracist multicultural education and feminist forms of thought have been found to be relevant. Disability is another form of oppression and, as such, disability awareness, like antiracism and antisexism, should be part of equal opportunity education and training. This has been a wide-ranging discussion underpinned by a belief that disabled people are unjustly treated and that this situation ought to change. It will not do so unless and until there is more recognition of this injustice.

As I mentioned earlier, for me Paul Abberley has convincingly argued that disability is a form of oppression (Abberley 1987). Most (perhaps all) serious disability is caused by social factors: war injury, car accidents, industrial injury, environmental pollution, medical consequences (e.g. whooping cough vaccine damage) and pre- and post-natal mishap. Thus, ironically, when, through prejudice or decisions about resources, disabled people are denied their rights (to access, to educational resources, to employment, etc.) we penalise the very people who are paying a price for the general public 'advantages' of our social, industrial, scientific and medical practices. The 'price' is the impairment, the loss of a function as the result (in almost all cases) of environmental hazards.

We often fail to recognise that disabled people are subject to the same kind of endemic prejudice and institutionalised discrimination as other oppressed social groups. There is an unspoken assumption that, though black people and women are equal to whites and men, 'the disabled' are inferior to 'normal' people.

As individuals we each have a range of abilities and disabilities. We label people as disabled if their disability is sufficiently handicapping. Yet, as we have seen, the degree to which a disability is a handicap depends upon the social context in which we function.

The 'disability awareness' in education which I shall advocate means enabling all children to understand the ways in which disabled people are devalued and denied their rights.

I am aware that talk of 'oppression' may appear to some people to be rather extreme, unnecessarily confrontational and counter-productive. However, certainly in the context of disability, the word or idea is in effect a kind of shorthand for the recognition of the amalgam of the points made by Abberley and others. 'Oppression' is a concise way of referring to the combination and interaction of endemic prejudice and stereotyping on the one hand, and negative discrimination (in education, employment, income, social arenas, etc.) on the other. This dangerous combination adversely affects the quality of people's lives to the extent that, as a group, disabled people are materially substantially disadvantaged. It is my hope that those not convinced of this will become more convinced by reading the experiences of the people 'speaking' in the chapters to come. It may well be that 'oppression' will no longer seem too radical a description of the factors and social forces which they describe.

Towards an Enabling Education

The negative attitudes and discrimination experienced by our respondents endorsed an important finding of our earlier research into equal opportunity practice in university departments, namely that there is a relative lack of awareness of disability as a form of oppression and correspondingly little 'disability awareness' in departmental practice and provision – both in terms of the general curriculum (for all students) and in terms of catering for special needs. To achieve such disability awareness requires a process of equal opportunity education/training to sensitise educators and others to the prejudice and discrimination experienced by disabled people.

I have argued elsewhere (Leicester 1996) that there are four aspects of the equal opportunity ideal:

1. *A basic conception of equal opportunities*: to promote policies and practices which eliminate or avoid some of the current direct and indirect unfair discrimination in education. And 'fairness' is not always about same treatment or equal distribution. To treat people equally means treating them equally well and this often means not treating them the same. Equal medical treatment would not entail the same quantity of drugs for each patient but would entail equally good medical care for each one.

2. *A substantive conception of equal opportunities*: to promote policies and practices which would lead to greater ability and motivation in those who currently have (relatively) less.

3. *A liberal conception of equal opportunities*: to promote the development of respect for all people.

4. *A radical conception of equal opportunities*: to promote equality for social groups as social groups, for example through the use of quota systems.

An education that provides more equal opportunities for disabled children and adults can only be achieved by considerable changes in our education system, including the kind of reorientation of the structures of provision and the curriculum which would affect the education of everyone. This could be compared with the kinds of change advocated, and to some extent achieved, by the Swann Report (1985) in relation to the education of children from minority ethnic groups. Again, I have argued elsewhere (Leicester 1992) that it may be necessary to politicise disability if the inclusion of disabled people in mainstream education is to be successful, so that the developments in the education of children with special needs may parallel the development of the inclusion of black children. This development moved from separation in separate language centres and so on, through integration into an unchanged, monocultural mainstream, to pluralism, to antiracism. Similarly, to achieve inclusion we must move from segregation in special schools and so on, through ill-prepared integration into unchained mainstream schools to planned, well-resourced inclusion based on a recognition of all children's right to a broad, balanced, relevant curriculum without social segregation.

I shall call the idea of an education which both provides a disability-aware education for all and which caters adequately for everyone's (special) educational needs, across the life-span, *an enabling education*. What aims would this education have?

Such an education would:

1. Provide equal educational opportunities for disabled people at school and post-school stages.

2. Ensure that disabled children and adults would not be marginalised from mainstream education. Within the mainstream their educational needs and interests would be fully catered for.

3. Ensure that all children would receive a disability-aware education. They would not continue to acquire prejudice about disabled people through the schooling process.

4. Ensure that disability awareness permeates formal and informal adult education, that is, permeates adult programmes of study and informs the mass media and other agents of our informal learning.

Having listened, in the coming chapters, to the voices of disabled people, in the light of their experiences and views, in the final chapter we shall explore what might be done towards realising these four aims. Thus it is to the achieving of a more enabling education that what follows seeks to make a small contribution.

CHAPTER 2

The Social Context

Education takes place in a social context and though our respondents were aware that our research focus was on education, they were keen to discuss that wider context too. Significant shared non-educational experiences emerged; that is, experiences not directly connected with education, but which, as our respondents often pointed out, had educational implications. For example, the poor communication almost universally reported in relation to the diagnosis of impairment clearly has implications for the professional education and training of those in health care and other relevant professions.

Many non-educational experiences had informed our interviewees' opinions about education. Thus the experience of negative public attitudes towards impairment, which was shared by *all* our respondents, tends to highlight the need for a more disability-aware public education. Such an omission from much current educational provision may simply not be noticed by those who have not been exposed to endemic public prejudice of this kind.

There were four main arenas of 'non-educational' experiences that emerged as significant: (1) the experience of the process of diagnosis; (2) the experience of gaps in resources and in information about resources; (3) the experience of negative attitudes from the public and sometimes from within the family; and (4) the experience (positive and negative) of disability as a dimension of a meaningful life.

Problems about resources and about public prejudice (Arenas 2 and 3) affect all aspects of the daily lives of disabled people; thus, though they are problematic features of disabled living outside of education, they do also (as we shall see in Chapters 3 and 4) infect the educational experience too.

Arena 1: Life Crisis and Communication

Not surprisingly, for many people the diagnosis of impairment, whether an impairment of their own or of their baby or child, is often experienced as a life crisis. It is a shock and a blow to have to assimilate the fact that one will not see again or will not walk again or must face an illness that will progressively impair. This is why, as was discussed in the previous chapter, laudable recognition of the social nature of disability should be complemented by an empathetic understanding that impairment often brings suffering to the individual concerned and their family and friends – some the unnecessary and inhumane result of prejudice (e.g. name calling and social isolation) and some the less avoidable outcome of adjusting to the loss of a function or coping with physical pain. For all our respondents, diagnosis (and for almost all, the poor quality of the communication of it) had been one of their most distressing experiences.

It seems extremely sad that the poor quality of the process and communication of a diagnosis, for our respondents, added to their suffering at such a critical time. The trauma of the actual diagnosis was exacerbated both by poor communication about it and by lack of follow-up counselling or support.

Poor Listening Skills

Many of our respondents had experienced 'not being listened to'. Doctors and others had not taken symptoms seriously, and this sometimes had delayed diagnosis with adverse medical consequences:

> Well, she was about 8 lbs when she was born and I used to take her every couple of weeks to the welfare clinic to be weighed, like you do. And she was known there as a model baby 'cause she did everything absolutely on time and all that. But then when she was about 18 months old she started to stumble rather a lot, and I was a bit worried about that. So I took her to the welfare people and they told me that she was doing it for attention. I went home and at first when I was coming out of the clinic I felt quite happy. Then I thought, 'I don't believe it, 'cause why should a perfectly happy, secure little girl suddenly start falling over and hurting herself for attention?' And I talked about it that evening with my cousin who happened to be there doing some electrical work and with the man I lived

with, and they both said, 'I think you should go to the doctor tomorrow', which I did, to my own GP. He immediately got [her] into the children's hospital for an exploratory operation, so if I'd listened to the welfare people, and left it a whole fortnight, it would have been very very serious to do that. And this is a common experience. I know from talking to other mothers in the hospital, it was very common that they weren't listened to. The assumption is that mothers are making an undue amount of fuss or worrying unnecessarily, whereas, if only they would listen more, things would happen more promptly, and it would be good. Anyway, it turned out that when she was operated on she had a malignant brain tumour and it was very malignant and would have to have surgery and then radiotherapy, so she had an operation that took a very long time to remove the tumour and then she had to go into Christie Hospital, cancer hospital, for radiotherapy.

In the most extreme example of this commonly reported experience, one grandmother describes how her daughter, in seeking help for her brain-damaged baby, was simply seen as an 'anxious mother' and herself given psychiatric care:

Grandmother: He had difficulty in feeding ... consequently he was losing weight ... about two months of age he started to fit. We didn't realise it was a fit, it was like a startled reaction that babies have. But he did it quite frequently and his chin used to come down on to his chest. Now she was at the doctors nearly every week with the baby, and they got her down as an anxious mother ...

Interviewer: So they didn't appreciate that he'd got problems?

Grandmother: We weren't believed. The medical profession didn't see it, so they decided to put the mother into the psychiatric ward at Walsgrave with the baby.

All but one of the parents had experienced this unwillingness to take their worries seriously. Many of our adult respondents had been too young to remember their diagnoses but, unfortunately, those facing impairment in later life told a similar story.

For example, this young adult describes how she was 'told' about her multiple sclerosis:

> It was the most appalling process I have ever been through; it was terrible. I mean all that sort of going back to the doctor and saying, 'There is a problem. What is happening?' and then just telling me it is stress. And I was getting to the stage where I was thinking, 'Well perhaps it is stress', because I was feeling so depressed, but I was thinking, 'Why don't you send me to someone to see about that, a counsellor?' because it was getting so much. And then the actual process of telling me in hospital was terrible. I think they have a real fear of telling anyone that there is something seriously wrong with them. They don't know how to handle it.

One adult respondent vividly remembered how difficult she had found it to be listened to as a child, even by her mother:

> Whenever I tried to talk about it or get them to listen to me it was always something I was doing wrong. It was always ... you're feeling tired, you don't sleep until late at night, that's why you're feeling tired. You've got a headache because you don't eat properly or you have got to wear gloves because when you wash and stuff, that's why you're getting these cuts. There was always something I was responsible for ... Sometimes I think I was probably resentful that nobody was listening and then you end up just keeping it to yourself. And it's something that I threw up in my mum's face for years afterwards. You know, like when I did become very ill, I used to say, 'Well, remember when I used to tell you about the swelling in my shoulder and you wouldn't take me seriously because you thought I was skiving off school?'

Poor Communication Skills

It was clear, then, from the vast majority of interview transcripts, that there is a widely shared and frustrating experience of not being listened to, sometimes delaying diagnosis of a serious condition. However, also of concern is that even when doctors and others were very well aware of a patient's condition, poor communication about this added to shock, distress and misunderstanding. Here are some examples.

MISUNDERSTANDING

The doctor just said at the end, 'We think she's going to be all right.' Now as a mother you immediately think, 'all right, good', don't you? So whether he meant he really did think she was going to be all right, or whether he meant she was going to be *physically* all right, … which thinking about it since maybe that's what he meant. I mean physically she was developing perfectly normally, but having said that to a mother, 'all right' means 'all right'.

DIFFICULTY IN OBTAINING INFORMATION

They were sensitive in a way. They were probably at times too sensitive, you know? Because we just wanted to know what her outcome was. But we found we were getting the information in dribs and drabs, you know? Me and my husband just wanted somebody to come straight out and tell us what was happening with her, but the nurses wouldn't tell us anything because they are not allowed to really, and they kept saying 'oh, you'll have to wait to see the doctor', which was, I thought, a bit frustrating. I don't see why the nurses can't tell you what they know. I mean they'll probably tell you in more detail that you can understand better [than the doctor] anyway … Eventually, one of the nurses, she had to insist on the doctor coming to speak to us.

This Asian mother had the courage for the sake of other mothers to tell the paediatrician about the poor way in which he gave her the information that her new baby had Down's Syndrome:

> And I said to him, 'The way you gave me the news was wrong. It would have helped if you'd broken the news gently.' And I said, 'Initially you should have waited for my husband to be there because it's his baby as well. My husband's, not just mine, and told us together … for some sort of comfort.' And I said 'If he wasn't there, all right, at least you could have sat near me and held my hand or put your arm around my shoulder or something, and told me gently.' And do you know what he said to me? He said, 'Well, some Indian women are peculiar.' I'll never forget that. And he said, 'They don't like somebody holding their hand, and that sort of thing,' he said to me. I said, 'It's a nice way, just holding her hand and telling her.' I don't think any Indian woman would mind. Even if a doctor held my mum's hand. She's much older than me, obviously, of a different

generation, but she wouldn't mind. I said, 'No matter what colour a woman is, at this time … when you have such news, she needs some sort of comfort, some sort of sympathy.

A very small percentage of those interviewed (10%) reported more positive experiences at these difficult moments of the communication of the diagnosis. Thus one mother described her experience like this:

I had to wait and see Dr B and she was very good and she waited 'til the evening; she made the excuse that she had to wait to get a stethoscope that obviously she didn't need, but she wanted to wait until my husband was there with me. And she got us into an office with another nurse and with our baby there, with us as well, and she told us, and she was really good and she dealt with it very sensitively, and she let us have time to cry and ask questions. And I really felt that it was dealt with very well indeed. And they even let my husband stay with me that night in the private room, which was really nice, what I really needed. And then when we got home she came to see us, to talk to us, and we could ask any questions we liked, even stupid questions, which we did, and I was very pleased with how we were treated and I know that I am one of the few. In fact, I don't know anybody else that could actually say that. I really feel that I'm the only person, and I spoke to many, many mothers and they've all been treated very badly, even their husbands not being there with them, or they've just been told as if it's nothing, just a cold or something. So I think, I feel very sort of fortunate that I was treated that way.

A woman who developed multiple sclerosis described how it was her husband from whom she learned of her condition, thus enabling a more sympathetic approach:

Well it was after I was married, and my husband took me upstairs. My parents were downstairs. They had come to visit us. He said, 'You've got something that many other people have got' and I was so relieved to hear that about other people. I was not an oddity. 'You mean other people have got what I have got?' And he said, 'You have got something called MS.' I hadn't even heard of it. Well, perhaps I had heard of it with Jacqueline du Pré. Then I said, 'Well who can I contact?' and he gave me the name of a very nice lady, Carol, and I phoned her up. She was a jolly person. She came

round and introduced me to other people with the same disability and you realised that they were just normal people who very unfortunately had this horrible disease that they couldn't get rid of and there is no cure for at present. *At present!* But lots of people are working on it, and who knows?

Unequal Power Relationships

It seems, then, that communication of a diagnosis is not always done with empathy and clarity. It also emerged that a complicating factor was the unequal power relationship between professional and patient: 'They are like god ... and their bedside manner, some of them, is awful, and it's a power thing ...'

Trusting the doctor seems sometimes to mean not being given the opportunity to know:

> It was quite a long process of finding out that I was ill. What happened was that I started to notice when I was about 20, 21, I would have periods when I would be extremely tired, and I would have things like pins and needles, and at one stage my arm went very weak, and I would think that all of these things were slightly strange. I would go along to the doctors and say that I had got these problems, and they would say, 'Given your age it is probably stress, don't worry about it.' I didn't know at the time, why they kept doing all these strange tests. I wondered why they were doing them, but I just thought 'The doctors know.' So I just went away and after about a month or so the symptoms would disappear. So this went on over about four years. I would have periods when I would be ill and I would go to the doctors and go through the same process. And then it got worse and I got fairly worried about it, and I started to get very down psychologically. I was very depressed. I went back to the doctors and at this stage I didn't just think, 'Well, it will go away in a month or so.' I kept going back to the doctors every few weeks ...

Lacking medical knowledge and feeling ill, many patients are not in a good position to be assertive. This interviewee describes how it was her brother, himself a doctor, who was able to secure the early appointment she needed. (Many patients, of course, do not have such an advocate.)

Basically he said I couldn't be admitted into hospital on the National
Health Service for possibly up to four or five weeks but my family could
choose to go private if they wanted to. And I think he wasn't really
listening to what I was saying, you know, all the things I was suffering
from. And I think because my brother had a medical background he was
assertive and he just said, 'I don't care about the National Health Service, I
just want her seen by a specialist and I want for her to have medical
attention now.' And what happened was the next day I got an appointment
with the consultant because normally you have to go through the
procedure of him writing to them and then them sending you the
appointment.

A small number of people read up the relevant literature for themselves:

And within a week I had read up every single piece of literature I could
about it and not just about the various effects but once you had read it,
scales fell from before your eyes and you wonder, 'Well why didn't anyone
tell me about this before?' Like the problem of tightness in my limbs. You
think, God Almighty, if I'd known this two or three years ago. Since then I
have read about diet but that was self taught – you go by the books. But no
one had ever said a thing.

This unequal power relationship may sometimes prevent full professional
recognition of how much disabled people themselves know about impairment and its consequences and treatment:

I think it's a shame that a lot of professional people don't respect the fact
that you've lived with whatever and therefore you know what you're
talking about when you're trying to explain about spasm and things and
it's very difficult because you actually know a lot more about it than others
and people aren't always willing to listen and accept that. Yes, you're the
patient or the client or whatever it is, and you have some knowledge, and
reading it from books is quite different from actually living it, and I think
it's a shame that there isn't a way in which if somebody wants to they could
be helped to give something back to the profession. There isn't an
automatic acceptable way.

Diagnosis and Communications: Tentative Conclusions

Of course, as we see in some of the extracts above, some doctors and other health professionals are sensitive, kind and communicate well. Nor must we underestimate the often complex and difficult nature of both diagnosis and its communication. It may be that diagnosis is not always incompetent just because it seems so. For example, it may sometimes need to be protracted. Nor does patient misunderstanding always indicate poor communication on the doctor's part. However, the *frequency* of complaint about aspects of diagnosis and communication should give cause for concern. It seems, for example, that mothers are too readily perceived as over-anxious rather than as likely to have some substantive cause for their concern. It seems, too, that good practice to communicate difficult news is not always followed (e.g. giving the opportunity for the individual to be accompanied by their partner or a friend). Nor was there any automatic structure such that diagnosis led to useful information about support services, or networks, or allowances, or aids available in connection with a particular impairment.

Diagnosis and its communication are difficult and important tasks for doctors and other health care workers. They deserve support for these tasks in the form of a professional training which includes disability awareness and communication skills, particularly as a professional culture may encourage a lack of appreciation of non-professionals' direct knowledge of the effects of disability on everyday life.

Arena 2: The 'Catch 22' of Resources

By 'resources' for disabled people, I mean any one of a number of kinds of assistance or provision. These include financial assistance (benefits, allowances, grants, etc.); emotional support (guidance, counselling, empathetic listening, support groups, etc.); aids (medical and environmental); and special services and provision (special training courses, resource centres, assistants, etc.). It could be argued that these resources are currently inadequate. Disability welfare benefits tend to be set at fairly basic levels, for example. And even where specific need is clearly identified, resources to meet these needs may be limited. For instance, our parent respondents found that needs detailed in their child's statement (see Chapter 3) were often inadequately met because the school lacked the financial resources to ensure otherwise.

When decisions are made about the allocation of a society's resources, how often do those making the decisions reflect that the environmentally caused impairments of disabled people are, therefore, almost always caused by the scientific, medical and technical 'progress' which benefits us all? And how often are disabled groups consulted, and how often are disabled individuals part of the decision-making group?

Given that resources tend to be inadequate, it is doubly unfortunate that even those which exist are often not of benefit to many relevant individuals, because they *do not know* about them. People cannot ask for, or about, benefits or contacts or services which they have no reason to know exist. This is the 'Catch 22' of resources. Certainly the experience of our respondents was that crucial forms of support were not always available and that where there were relevant resources to be had, they had not learned of them until well past the point when they could have benefited from them. I say 'could have benefited' both in the sense that had people known about the resource, it would have been useful earlier in their life, and in the sense that they would have been entitled to it at that earlier point. The information about resources tended to reach individuals late, in an *ad hoc* manner, often through chance encounters or remarks. The following extracts provide examples of these problems about resources:

LATE FINANCIAL BENEFITS AND ALLOWANCES

I do find that because I tend to make light of problems, that maybe I didn't get things quite so early.

MISINFORMATION

I'm having a bit of a problem at the moment, still not getting the mobility allowance. When I phoned up for a form the chap on the phone said that my daughter should automatically get it and I didn't need a form. And I waited and waited and nothing happened so I wrote a letter, didn't hear anything, wrote another one and then they sent me another form. But part of it I've got to get the doctor to fill in, I've only just had it recently but I mean I don't know why that chap told me that I didn't need a form and then we did, you know?

NO INFORMATION

Well, what I would say about welfare is, I've now come to feel that whatever I can get for my daughter I will get for her, and that it is a right and not a charity, I feel that very strongly. I also feel, all of her growing up we never had any welfare benefits, because nobody ever told me that they were available and I mean, I've never actually felt poor, but that's a personal thing about something about the way I am. I have actually nevertheless had very low income, you know. I mean I resigned my job when my daughter was ill, to look after her. And a few years later [I] got divorced, so I've not always had a good income, although I've never felt poor. But nobody thought to tell me that there might be certain benefits I was entitled to, like attendance allowance. So all of my daughter's growing up we didn't have various things we were entitled to, simply because we didn't have the information. And I think on behalf of other disabled people that it is worth saying that there should be much more information about people's entitlements, because they are rights, not charities, and people ought to know about them. And a lot of welfare benefits simply aren't taken up to the degree they could be simply because people don't know about them, because there's nothing built into the system where they automatically get to know about them. I mean even though she was going to a special school I didn't know about these things …

★ ★ ★

People don't know that they can get extra allowances for personal care, and you don't do things, not to be a burden on your family. So, many disabled people just sit at home with their families and think their families have to help because they don't know about personal care allowances.

★ ★ ★

My experience, even to this day, is that blind students are not [as] informed as they should be about the facilities available to them. I don't know why they're not but they seem to me not to be informed.

★ ★ ★

A lot of people don't know about the benefits and it's not fair. Nobody is talking to us about it. We have got to pay bills.

When I actually couldn't drive using normal pedals I didn't know about hand controls for quite a long time. It wasn't until, just by accident, somebody said, 'You know there is a place that you can go and get hand controls and you'll be able to drive'. And yet I had no idea about that. And so it's that lack of knowledge that is around.

Where people felt that they had received good information promptly, and assistance in obtaining the resources required, often a home teacher or social worker had been invaluable.

Yes, I had a home teacher, and she was brilliant, and I think unusual in the fact that she supported us in every way. She was like a social worker as well as a teacher, and she gave us welfare advice and benefit advice, everything. She even brought the forms in for us, everything, you know. And various appointments I had to go to, to do with other things, like hearing problems and what have you, she took us, actually took us there herself personally. She didn't have to. I didn't have any transport and it was not only the transport but also the support from her. And I think that that was again very unusual – G.H. was very unique in that respect, and I wonder how many of us parents are getting that support. Because obviously that's not her job description. She's just a home teacher, and she's doing it out of the kindness of her heart.

* * *

We've been very lucky at PAC [Parent Action Committee] where we went to. There was a social worker on hand who, when the child got to the right age for the welfare, they would come and give you all the information going. So we've been brought a lot of the details.

ON COUNSELLING

Nobody ever suggested that I was depressed or offered me valium or anything like that, but now I recognise that I was in quite deep depression for quite a long time. Whether I would have been better if I'd been on any counselling or psychiatric treatment or whether that would have made things worse, because somebody had put a mental health label on me, as well as a lack of physical health, I don't know, but I wasn't.

* * *

I was never offered any counselling. And I really felt I needed it because I was quite desperate.

Almost all of the mothers of disabled children mentioned the lack of counselling *after* diagnosis. Several of the mothers suggested that it would have been very useful to have been put in touch with another mother who had been through a similar experience:

I wish that they'd sent another mum who had a Down's child. If a mum had come to see me at the hospital and told me, 'Look, you know, it's not the end of the world. It's not what you think'; just a little positive thing. That would have made me feel a lot better.

Of course, just as not all material resources are relevant for each (unique) individual, so not everyone felt that they needed or wanted counselling. It would be a mistake to assume this.

I received tremendous support from my colleagues and from my wife, tremendous, wonderful, but I never asked for or received any personal support. I mean on the day when I was registered blind at the Birmingham and Midland Eye Hospital, I think it was that day, I was introduced to the rehabilitation social worker, who gave me a range of information which was intended to be of a very helpful kind, but none of which was relevant to my needs. The only use I made of the official support agencies was that I found out there was a shop that sold artefacts for blind people and my wife drove me there and I bought a white cane. That, I think, was the only support I got or sought! I bought a white cane, that was it.

ON HOUSING ...

And he [my disabled grandson] stayed with me then, which was very difficult, because I was in a one-bedroomed flat in town which had stairs to it. It was very difficult. We used to carry up, from the car, the shopping and our boy. So I plagued the council straight away, and now, after some years, I've got a council flat. In modifying the flat for him I had [an] £860 grant, I think, and it cost me £2000 because of all the sliding doors and things like that. I found well over £1000 for it myself.

In discussing resources and provision, some of our respondents gave examples of gaps in current provision and made suggestions for useful developments, including better transport provision for disabled people and more adequate public leisure facilities. For example, the mothers of disabled children felt that public play areas for children could be more consciously designed to cater better for disabled children.

Arena 3: Patterns of Prejudice

It is widely recognised that there are endemic social prejudices about disabled people. Such recognition is encapsulated, for example, in the radio programme title: 'Does he take sugar?', which arises from a wide-scale experience of being ignored, of being treated as unable to make decisions and to speak for oneself. For instance, those being pushed in their wheelchair often find that members of the general public address only the wheelchair pusher, even to ask questions about the wheelchair user him- or herself.

At a common-sense level, 'prejudice' is often defined in terms of making a 'pre-judgement'. This captures an important feature of prejudice – its irrational nature. Any member of a group about whom we have a prejudice will tend to be judged without regard to evidence. We make a prior judgement that this individual will have certain negative attributes which we associate with that group. When these negative attributes or images are so prevalent as to constitute a stereotype, they are readily reinforced by the mass media. Thus social prejudices are easily acquired but much less easily unlearned. They are easily acquired because of the force of common stereotypes; they are not easily unlearned because there often seems to be an emotional component to our deep-seated prejudices which tends to make us resist rational argument and evidence. Moreover, we find it painful to acknowledge our prejudice.

There is a wealth of evidence that there are endemic, deep-seated social prejudices about various social groups (black groups, gay people, women, etc.) which have their roots in a variety of historical, economic and psychological factors. However, because most people feel sympathetic about impairment, they often do not recognise society's and their own deeper prejudices about disabled people.

I have found that when I have written about oppressed groups, such as black people, women and disabled people, experiencing endemic social prejudice, this has been described as racist and sexist. 'After all,' goes the argument, 'there is nothing intrinsically wrong with black people or women.' This is, of course, true. There isn't. But the implication that there *is* something wrong with disabled people is a dangerous one which too readily generalises an impairment to the whole person. Thus the person is then implicitly assumed to be of less worth. He or she is *devalued*.

Such prejudices are harmful because they adversely affect the quality of the lives of those subject to them. Because prejudices affect our thinking, our speaking and our actions, they are linked to negative discrimination against members of disfavoured groups. Such discrimination, being widespread and large scale, works to the substantial material disadvantage of disabled people – in terms of employment opportunities, for example. Disabled people also bear the brunt of prejudiced beliefs and assumptions in their day-to-day encounters.

Our respondents described many such hurtful interactions. Their experience confirms the endemic nature of prejudice against the disabled and reveals some of the pattern of this prejudice; that is, some of the common forms in which it is manifested and in which it impacts on daily life.

Staring and Name Calling

The experience of being stared at because of being 'different' or of people looking quickly away are common, unpleasant experiences of those who are perceived to look different from the recognised and approved norms:

> I remember when she was in college, she wrote a poem called 'Why do people stare at me?' And she's also always had people make nasty comments to her just in the street, and she'll come home quite upset ... that somebody quite gratuitously has said something about her lack of hair, or her height, or her fatness or something like that. She's less upset these days, only because she's learnt this coping strategy of regarding it as their problem. I've said to her, 'If people are nasty to other people like that, I think they are just very unhappy people, who are taking it out on other people.' And she's kind of accepted that, and she sees it as their problem, and she'll even say to them sometimes, 'You must be very unhappy if you go round making nasty remarks to people.' So she's found a way of coping with it.

* * *

They sort of stare at the back of my head and before I actually had this hair plaited into the back of my head, people would turn round, stare, call rude names, you name it.

* * *

Normal able-bodied people, they look at you sometimes as if you have got two heads. They do.

And we have been to places in town and we've been sitting there and people have been looking over and my daughter would be saying, 'God, look at the lady staring over.' I don't think half the time people mean to be nasty by staring, you know.

* * *

She was bounding about like a three-year-old because she gets excited, she still does it now, people turn and stare. So you did get that sort of thing sometimes. Most people were very good, I must admit. We didn't have an awful lot of problems but you did get the odd staring, and I'd much rather people would come up and ask me, rather than stare.

* * *

The attitude towards disabled people in today's society makes it harder for us because we get looked at, we get stared at, and we get called names by them, and all the rest of it. But they don't get called names by their friends do they? So, I mean, why should we get called names, just because of something different about us? I've often said to my mum, 'It's not us that's disabled, in fact, it's them, because of the way they look at us.'

* * *

Hurtful remarks are sometimes made to other members of the disabled person's family: 'A little lad up the road keeps saying to one of my daughters "Your sister's a spastic" and all that, and I say, "Just take no notice."'

FEAR OF DISABILITY

They must be frightened of it because why else would they do it? I can't understand their reactions but it must be for that reason, that they're frightened of it, because they've never come across people with disabilities before. They've always been used to people who've got no disability whatsoever, like themselves, so of course they come across these people with disabilities and it frightens them.

PATRONISATION

They either ignore you or pat my hand and say 'Good boy.' Oh it's bad news all round but what can we do about it?

'Normalisation'

Because of these negative experiences, several of our respondents sought to hide or minimalise their disability, making efforts to appear 'normal'. Two individuals mentioned having to pretend all was well ('put on a brave face' and 'put on a false me'). It is all too easy to stigmatise people as moaners or as aggressive or as 'having a chip on their shoulder' when they may be expressing legitimate grievances and understandable frustrations.

We had a guy, he's a first year and he's got one arm. He's missing a hand and he's got one arm shorter than the other. He's had a few problems but he doesn't like people to know he's disabled so he keeps his arm in his jacket all day and therefore he can't write his notes and he can't use the computer and he's falling behind.

* * *

I used to put on a brave face for people, but at that time I was having problems like walking across campus, putting on clothes, making myself something to eat and even actually eating because my swallowing mechanism was going. So I was experiencing all those problems but I would put on a brave face. If people said to me, friends said to me, 'Let's go out and eat' I would always pretend I'd eaten already.

* * *

In the normalisation process I am right at the bottom. I'm an alien, a woman and old. You've ageism, you've got genderism, you've got everything and with a disability it's like an extra label on you. And then with a white cane it seems to me like it's a label. I found it hard when I go out into the community, how people want to perceive me, with a white stick, it's like a label for me.

I could be myself with my friends, yes, but with a lot of the tutors when I was in my teens, I often used to think, 'Well I'll have to put on a false me. I'll have to pretend that I'm happy, even though I'm not', you know? So that's what I did, but I've coped with every situation as and when it comes because I feel that that's the only way you can do it really.

The Double Bind of 'Public Perception'

It's really funny, I applied for a mortgage recently and I had to let them know about my disability or my illness and they sent me off to have a medical with a doctor. I dressed, you know, really summery and like sporty, almost like learning to play the game. I was quite up front about my illness, and saying generally I lead a fairly normal life, but you are still penalised. I mean, I am having to pay on my life insurance three times as much as the normal person, and that's intriguing. Especially when you can justifiably go for something like mobility allowance, but if you look fairly OK, well, they're going to say we are not going to give it to you.

Inappropriate Behaviour

Some forms of inappropriate behaviour seem inexcusable:

Four years ago I broke my arm and I went into hospital. I needed a week or so until I could literally get into the chair so I could come home. This is absolutely true. I was asleep. It was the middle of the night, my first night after being shunted from Leicester, where it happened, to Coventry, absolutely knackered, and I was woken up with the light going on above me. It was a doctor and he said, 'I just wanted to have a look at you,' and he pulled the sheets down. And I said, 'Sorry, what's going on?' I said 'What's wrong?' He said, 'Oh you came in yesterday didn't you?' and I said 'Yes', and he said 'You don't mind if I have a look at you because what you've got is very, you know, unusual and just ...' And I think that is outrageous, and he was asking me what it was called. And I said, 'Well, you're the doctor.' And I was getting angry, and he was saying, 'There's no need to be like that.' And I said, 'Well, what time is it? Why are you doing this?' He said, 'I'm just interested.' So I said, 'Why don't you come to me tomorrow and *ask* me?' I don't think you can use that sort of excuse. A lot of medical people do that.

Some inappropriate behaviour is well meaning, but if disabled people were less segregated as children (see Chapter 3) we might all have learned more useful responses. Many people wish to be helpful to others and would be more enabled in this with a more disability-aware education:

> They are just students trying to be helpful, which is nice. I mean I don't resent that, and I always reply in a perfectly friendly manner. When I get into the lift a student will often say, 'Where are you trying to go to?' and I just press the button for the third floor and say, 'The third floor, where are you trying to get to?' I try not to be rude, but sometimes you have to be just a little bit forceful.

> I occasionally encounter this thing, all blind people do, where you approach the door at the end of your corridor, and it's not there. You go through it without realising you've gone through it. So you re-trace your steps just to make sure it was there and you assume that perhaps there's been a back up against it and you find there's a human being standing there, stiff against the wall, holding it open for you. And you touch this human being who then says, 'Oh, um, sorry, I was holding the door open for you.' And then I have to say, 'Oh, sorry.' Particularly if I touch them in an inappropriate part of their anatomy! And then I normally say, 'Thank you very much. Next time you see me go past, just greet me will you, and tell me you're holding the door open for me, that would help me a lot.' I mean you get that, people just don't quite know how to behave, that's all, and they learn, don't they, through experience?

In situations when the individual is known, much more 'accepting' attitudes tend to prevail:

> The majority reaction is one that I am completely taken for granted, indeed people often forget I'm blind. The colleagues that I work with on a day-to-day basis are so used to me that I don't even think it bothers them and sometimes it doesn't even occur to them.

Negative Assumptions

Negative assumptions about disability are common. This parent points out that social attitudes about disability and abortion provide a graphic example of entrenched prejudice:

> I have people come up to me saying, 'What a shame, did you have the blood tests to find out?' And I say 'No, I didn't want any tests.' And they [can't] understand that, and they [think] that if they [had] had the tests they definitely would have had an abortion. Whereas ... I've spoken to mothers of Down's Syndrome children that said if they'd had the blood test, they would have had an abortion and they are just so glad that they didn't have the test because they love their child so much, and they are so rewarding. So this is the thing that really does bug me. The testing and the fact that you're not given any balanced advice when you do have the test, you know? It's a very negative view that you're given as a parent. I've even known a mother to be told by a doctor that she possibly could be carrying a Down's Syndrome child and that, ... 'You must realise they can break up families', and that was really upsetting for them. OK, you've got to sort of tell the parents some of the things that can be difficult with having a disabled child or a child with learning difficulties, but I think there should be a balanced view, and there are so many negative views. In the paper they have got ... headlines like: 'Good News for Down's Syndrome', and you look at it and all it is is a test so they can detect Down's Syndrome earlier so they can abort earlier and they are saying, 'Isn't that good news?' And that ... to me is so upsetting.

Arena 4: Dimensions of Disabled Living

At the end of each interview we asked each of our respondents to share with us some of their most positive and their most negative experiences. What they recounted in response were not so much specific incidents as positive and negative dimensions of their life as a disabled person or as the parent of a disabled child.

For parents, the existence of their much loved child, the joy and meaningfulness he or she has brought to their lives, was more than compensation for the stress that negative social attitudes to disability also brought to the family. Very often very special bonds of love were forged as parent and child faced difficulties together. Parents also thought that their other children had become more loving and caring through their relationship with a disabled sibling:

> The most positive thing is we just love him to bits. This Down's Syndrome really becomes secondary to his being alive and well. And he brings a lot of joy into our family, and it's given a different dimension to his brother. His brother, I feel, has become a very caring boy.

More negatively, parents suffered with their children both in exposure to public prejudices and in pain and worry associated with life-threatening conditions:

> Well one thing that I didn't mention is that he has a heart problem and that's been very hard because we didn't know if he was going to live or die at one stage, and the stress of going through that and being at Birmingham Children's Hospital was enormous. It went on for quite a long time and I think it did put a bit of a stress on our marriage when he came out of hospital. However, we got through that, and now that he's well, you know, he's just our joy.

They also worried about their children's future – 'What will happen to her after I die?' And at a more mundane level, they hated the competitiveness, often encouraged by schools, which devalued their child for his or her lack of a particular skill or skills:

> The thing is the pressure when mothers get together. 'My son is doing such a degree' and 'I want my son, when he grows up, to be a doctor or a lawyer.' They never say, 'I want my son to be a good and happy person.'

The disabled adults were conscious of how much they had learned as a result of their experiences. This learning included the acquisition of new skills, but also, at a deeper level, new kinds of appreciation and new forms of consciousness. A blind respondent, for example, said: 'My other senses have become more sensitive. I have learned to appreciate things more, through a purifying and concentrating of consciousness.'

This theme of self-development occurred in many responses. Our respondents felt that they had developed an understanding of life's priorities and had developed empathy with the suffering of others:

I think I have become a better person. Having gone through the experience, if I think of myself before I was ill and I think about afterwards, I think it could be to make myself feel better to say, 'Well, okay, I have gone through this awful experience but at the same time I am a better person for it.' But you know, maybe I am kidding myself, but I think I have. I think I have become far more tolerant of people. I think I have become more understanding of people, and I think I also see things very differently. I see life very differently. A lot of priorities in life are very different and I generally see people who have got health problems very differently now than I would have done. I don't think I take all things for granted, especially about my health. I find on that very personal level I have gained a lot and I do see things very differently.

More negative was the experience of being consistently reminded of their 'disability'. Striking examples of this were given in the daily experience of being stared at and of being devalued as 'different', both touched on earlier. We shall also see, in Chapter 4, that in occupational terms, many of our respondents felt constantly reminded of their 'disability'. Many experienced unwarranted negative assumptions about their disability and pressures to consider disability-related work, regardless of whether this was an interest they had or not.

Almost all respondents also mentioned the impact of their disability on the family as a whole. Of course, there was positive as well as negative impact, but while our parent respondents emphasised that, contrary to public assumptions, they did not regard their disabled child as a burden, our disabled adults did bear the burden of concern about their loved ones being exposed to stress or public prejudice associated with their impairment. One man who had lost his sight in adulthood, for example, talked of being conscious 'that the burden of my blindness is borne by my closest loved ones'. He had 'received tremendous support from my colleagues and from my wife'. This final example combines the experience of being stared at and the consciousness of being constantly reminded of one's disability with this concern for the impact on siblings and parents:

Everywhere we went I seemed to be the centre of attention and that was difficult; that was difficult for me because of what my brother and sister felt. They couldn't go anywhere without ... we just wanted to mingle in, and I think I was more upset because, you know, we went through shops and you had little kids staring at me and saying out loud to their mum and dad. It upset my mum and dad a lot more than perhaps it did me. I think that was half the problem, and I'd been out with one or two able-bodied girls and again the worst part is being seen out, not for me, I only get embarrassed because of what they're feeling. That's probably the hardest part and, though I'm quite a placid guy, that does anger me sometimes, you know, not because of me, but how they're feeling. They should be able to go out with me and go out and just mingle into the background, especially [in] this day and age, but I can't ever see the situation arising where it will be any different.

Conclusions

In this chapter we have explored the wider social context in which education takes place, focusing on four aspects of this context, aspects which were experienced by our respondents as of particular importance in their lives. These aspects were the diagnosis, resources, public prejudice and emotional dimensions of disabled living. In summary, the key points which emerged from each aspect were as follows:

1. Diagnosis of disability had proved to be a painful life crisis exacerbated by poor communication of it together with little social support.

2. There is a Catch 22 situation concerning all kinds of resources. People are not routinely informed of their entitlement to such provisions as do exist.

3. There are endemic social prejudices which impact very negatively on the daily lives of disabled people. These prejudices are manifested in staring, name calling, verbal insensitivity, inappropriate behaviour, negative assumptions and direct discrimination.

4. Conversely, there are positive aspects to disabled living, particularly in the emotional, spiritual and moral dimensions of a meaningful life – in loving relationships, the development of empathy, recognition of interdependence, caring values and people-centred priorities.

As we move into the world of education in the next chapter, we see that these dimensions, particularly problems with a lack of information about resources and with negative attitudes, re-emerge strongly in that context.

CHAPTER 3

Schooling
'A Culture of Gratitude'

Obviously the issue of schooling was very immediate for the interviewed parents, almost all of whose children were, at the time of interview, being educated in special schools. They had experienced the process of statementing and they had particular experiences and views which they wished to recount about their child's school. They all shared strong views about the issue of integrating disabled children into mainstream schools and some talked about after-school activities and their child's future.

Though schooling was less immediate for our adult respondents, who had more to say about their post-school and training/careers advice/employment-related experiences (see Chapter 4), it was interesting to see what they remembered with the perspective of time.

What follows is divided into three main issues: statementing, school experiences and integration. These important aspects of schooling, as one would expect, interrelate with the 'arenas' of Chapter 2 in that prejudiced attitudes and inadequate resourcing affect educational as well as non-educational social institutions and were key dimensions in the discussions about all three of the main issues. Lewis (1995) reports that children also describe experiences of prejudiced behaviour – bullying, kicking, teasing and name calling – particularly at playtime in mainstream schools.

Statementing

Legally, children in special schools, because they are deemed to have special educational needs, must have a statement made of those needs. Teachers, parents, doctors and educational psychologists must be involved in the assessment process leading up to the statement. Perhaps partly because parents are legally recognised as having a part to play in this assessment, they seem to have been given a genuine inclusion and voice in the process. Unlike in the experience of diagnosis and medical assessments, parents did not complain of not being listened to or of having felt disempowered or denigrated by professionals.

Statements are supposed to describe the special needs of the child, the special provision required to meet these and to name the school that will meet them. Several parents complained that though the description of special needs had been made, in fact the school had been unable to meet them. Here the resource issue re-emerges at a crucial point in the educational context. It appeared that a lack of resources (in the broadest sense) prevented the meeting of designated and agreed needs.

One parent described how her son, who had been deemed to need more water play, could only go in the school jacuzzi if she and another adult went in with him. There was no adult available at school to undertake this. As she could not often find someone to go with her, she was left feeling guilty that he was not receiving much of this (for him) crucial learning environment.

Similarly, another parent whose child was recognised as needing water play said:

> They have got a jacuzzi in that school, his own school, but we have to go to another one for the swimming. But that is shared by so many schools that we go in at 10.00 a.m. and there is another class comes in at 10.30 a.m. He only has half an hour a week. But we're very lucky to get that apparently. But it is a shame ...

Another mother said that her daughter's statement had specified physiotherapy and this, a health service provision, wasn't offered. She kept her child away from school in protest, until an arrangement was made: 'We had to fight for it, and the physio side by side with us had to fight. Even though it was identified in the statement that was what she needed. I mean it wasn't the school's fault you know. They didn't have the resources.'

This parental concern about resources in connection with statementing is shared by some schools. Some teachers feel that the local education authority (LEA) criteria for statutory assessment are becoming stricter, thereby reducing the numbers of pupils eligible for extra support by means of a statement (National Foundation for Educational Research (NFER) 1996). Some statements, where the needs identified required additional resources, were being issued without extra funding. Both schools and LEAs are worried about the balance between funding for pupils with statements and funding to cover the needs of pupils without statements, as the more statements that were issued, the less money there was available to support other pupils (NFER 1996). Thus a significant problem with current funding arrangements seems to be that the funding needs of those with and those without statements are, in effect, set in competition. Not only does this seem morally wrong, it is likely to distort our profiles of children's needs, with some professional pressure against statementing because of funding concerns. There are complex issues connected to funding and to the issue of statementing which are difficult to disentangle in a situation where we persist in seeing educational needs which deviate from the norm as somehow beyond, or additional to, our central obligations. Moreover, in such a situation, there is potential for conflict with parents who, seeking a resource needed by their child, exert pressure for a statement which might help them to secure it.

Three mothers mentioned the infrequency of the reviewing of statements. In theory there are annual reviews and parents are entitled to identify new needs, but in practice they do not always know this. It had not been clear, even to this mother of a disabled child who herself is a special school teacher, that there should be annual reviews of a child's statement. If she is confused it is not surprising that many parents pick up misinformation.

> I mean they are usually statemented when they are three for the provision that they need. But at three you don't actually know all their needs and you don't get a new revision until thirteen and a half ... I mean I was in special education and I didn't realise that I could actually make official representations because it's never explained to you.

A frequent complaint of parents is that the statementing process takes a long time. One mother, however, made interesting observations about the fact that assessment is made in a relatively short time considering that it is a very complex matter. It is tempting to slot children into neat categories, which, of course, they rarely fit:

> I'm always a bit funny about assessment because I can't see that in the very short time that they see them, they can actually 'get' the child really,

particularly one with peculiar problems like my daughter's got. I mean hers are not particularly straightforward in that she doesn't particularly fit any one category, and a lot of children don't.

The 1990 report of Her Majesty's Inspectorate (HMI) found considerable variation in the quality and use of statements across LEAs and many instances of lack of specificity. Our small number of respondents on this issue, though too small to be more than indicative, seems to confirm that statementing would be improved by more regular updating and requires more backing in terms of school resources to meet identified needs.

Code of Practice on the Identification or Assessment of Special Educational Needs

The need for a code of practice to guide schools in the identification and assessment of special educational needs arose in response to deficiencies in implementing the Education Act 1981, particularly the lack of provision for the 18 per cent of pupils identified by the Warnock Report (1978) as having special needs. The Code of Practice, introduced in 1994, is not a statutory instrument and, therefore, does not impose legal duties. However, each school must 'have regard to it' and it has raised the profile of special educational needs in mainstream schools. In addition to guidance about establishing a Special Educational Needs Co-ordinator (SENCO), a register and a school policy on special needs, it provides a useful staged approach to assessment in which needs should be met at each stage. It describes the procedures to be followed, within a strict timescale, in drawing up a statement of special educational needs and lays out plans for annual review arrangements. Responsibilities of LEAs and schools are set out and the need for consultation with pupils and parents is emphasised. The Code acknowledges that there is a continuum of needs, most of which will be met within the mainstream and without a statutory assessment. In order to be successfully met, however, such needs (the needs of approximately 18 per cent of mainstream pupils) should be identified and assessed as early as possible.

Setting up a register of pupils with special needs was a major task for many schools. In some LEAs the number of pupils listed on the register (usually at Stage Three) formed the basis for an audit on which the LEA allocated funding. Some schools found implementing the changes that the Code would require overwhelming; others that it matched the policies and procedures which they already had in place. (Insofar as the Code's guidance reflects the practice of those schools doing best by pupils with 'special educational needs', we shall return to it in considering our educational recommendations in the concluding chapter.)

A research project undertaken by the NFER (1995/96) (see Derrington, Evans and Lee 1996) explored the issues surrounding the implementation of the Code. The researchers found that it has had a significant effect on the work of LEAs and schools, though it remains to be seen whether it will have any long-term effect on the progress of pupils with special needs. In the short term, however, the Code does attempt to bring about a number of worthwhile changes:

- Pupils' difficulties and needs are being identified earlier.
- The formalisation of the role of SENCOs provides teachers with a source of information and guidance on how to identify and teach pupils with special needs.
- The introduction of the register allows schools and LEAs to monitor the progress of pupils in schools and the level at which support is being provided.
- Individual Education Plans, although at an early stage of development in some schools (particularly secondary schools), have the potential to draw teachers' attention to pupils' needs and how to meet them.
- LEAs and other agencies are working at improving their liaison so that schools and pupils will be provided with a more coherent and accessible service.
- Parents of pupils with special needs are becoming more involved in the decision-making process.
- An emphasis on including pupils in assessing and evaluating their own needs and progress.

The researchers remain concerned, however, about the lack of explicit criteria by which schools and LEAs can monitor the effectiveness of the provision they are making for pupils with special needs and about how resources for special needs are allocated to schools and how they are used to support pupils.

School Experiences

'Special Needs'

The notion of 'special needs' central to the process of statementing and, presumably, to the existence of special schools, is an interesting one. The Warnock Report defined 'special needs' in terms of learning difficulties which call for special educational provision. 'Learning difficulties' sometimes means that the child has significantly greater difficulties in learning than the majority of children of her or his age. It also sometimes means that the child has disabilities which prevent or hinder her or him from making use of educational facilities of a kind generally provided in LEA schools for children of that age. Thus the notion of 'learning difficulty' and of 'special needs' locates a deficiency with the child, a deficiency in terms of being different from the majority of children. Being in a minority is seen in terms of 'difficulty': the child is a problem!

Disabled children are no different from any other children in having a right and a need to be educated. How well or otherwise the schools are equipped to meet this common educational need varies in relation to children, since children are not all the same. Thus one might say that *schools* have learning/teaching difficulties in relation to some children – rather than locating the learning difficulty with the child.

However, it is probably fair to say that the Warnock Report at least sought to remove from schools the previously rigid and harmful categorisations (such as mentally or physically handicapped or educationally subnormal) by replacing these with the notion of 'learning difficulties' which could be 'mild', 'moderate' or 'severe'. Thus though the notions of 'learning difficulty' and, therefore, the notion of 'special need', are defined in terms of deviation from the norm (a potentially prejudicial way of thinking), it was generally seen as an improvement on offensive previous labels.

The conditions leading to learning difficulties cover a wide range, including physical disability, sensory impairment and low ability, as well as delicate, epileptic and gifted pupils and pupils with emotional and behavioural difficulties. It was estimated that about 20 per cent of pupils have some form of learning difficulty (special need) at some time in their schooling. (Of the total population of pupils with special needs, 63% are being educated in special schools, about 12% in special classes and 25% in mainstream classes. Some 1.3% of the total school population are educated in special schools and about 1.85% of the total school population have statements (OECD 1995).) Meeting these special needs was said to require one or more of the following:

- The provision of special means of access to the curriculum through 'special equipment', facilities or resources, modification of the physical environment or specialist teaching equipment.

- The provision of a special or modified curriculum.

- Particular attention to the social structure and emotional climate in which education takes place.

Special Schools

Almost all the children of the parents we interviewed were in special schools and some of our adult respondents had been educated in special schools. What follows represents their experiences and views of schooling, particularly in special education. Because the issue of 'integrating' disabled children into mainstream schools was the most frequently mentioned issue which people had clear and strong opinions about, it is dealt with in a separate section. At this point, rather, I have highlighted the factors about special schools that had been commonly experienced as advantageous or disadvantageous.

Many parents mentioned that their child enjoyed going to school and derived social benefits from being with other children:

> I think he's learnt to appreciate being with other children. He appreciates going to school because when the school bus comes he's quite happy, he wants to go. So that is progress. We don't get eye contact from C, [only] very very rarely, but I have noticed when we were swimming last week, we go in a circle, go round the swimming pool, and he was actually looking at Matthew, who said hello to him. And they were looking at each other, and he was giving him eye-to-eye contact, and I thought, 'this is great'.

* * *

She's with lots of kids, lots of people, which she does love; she loves to be with lots of people.

★ ★ ★

She's with a lot of kids. I mean she's very happy there you know. I've seen her with the kids. She's very happy, so my mind is at ease. I know she is happy; I've got time to spend with the baby and I look forward to having her home.

A smaller number of parents also said that their children were well stimulated at school and making good progress. (This contrasts with my own experience, which was that though my daughter was happy at special school, she was not as stretched academically as she could have been, and as she was at home.)

Now that he's gone to school it seems like he's on full throttle. He's coming out, he's started walking with a walking frame, he's now decided that he's very confident at climbing up and down the stairs and he's got speech. He's got speech, he's talking. And [it] comes across that he understands really really well everything that's going on, and then in another instance it's like you've got this tiny baby again, who'll just react by crying at things. But you can see the difference in him.

★ ★ ★

I feel very positive about the amount of time they spent with her getting her to walk. I mean, one of the education assistants used to walk for hours round the school with her, holding her little finger, trying to get her to let go.

One parent appreciated that her child's school was very supportive of parents:

They are very supportive to parents and they arrange a team morning twice a month where they invite all the parents and also anybody outside who wants to go. And they also have a parents' support group once a month, and they have speakers come in and you can go along, and the school is open. It feels very family orientated. The older children know the younger children and on their sports day it isn't the juniors doing their sports in the secondary, it's everybody in the hall together. Everybody partaking. It's very much the whole school as one, rather than this bit belongs here and this bit belongs there.

Another experience highlighted the importance of selecting an appropriate school for the particular child:

> You tend to be a one-off in a small school and your needs may not go with the rest of the group and that makes it very difficult. She has more youngsters around her that have language as well. I think, altogether, actually, she's thrived with the variety and size of the place really. She's not one of these youngsters that needs a very close sheltered environment and I think the original school was probably too small for her. She needs more space.

Some of our adult respondents had been educated in special schools and some in mainstream schools. When they were asked what they remembered about their schooling, interestingly they mainly commented on incidents reflecting prejudicial attitudes – one of the 'arenas' from the previous chapter as experienced in the educational context.

A mainstream school: 'I've had stick from people, but you get used to it. The important thing, when I started secondary school, initially I had a lot of trouble with other students.'

A special school: 'I used to hate going on a bus with the logo of the school on it. I could see the need for a bus that could take a chair etc. etc., but why all this logo? Who was that for? It drew attention … going down to Brighton you were watched.'

Some of the high-achieving adult respondents had become determined to succeed in the face of unhelpful attitudes: 'I said, "You're not going to make my life a failure because whatever happens, I'm going to succeed, because I've got the determination to succeed." And I said, "I'm just not letting people think they can walk over me and treat me the way that they do."'

Labelling

On the whole the parents mentioned the positive attitude of staff in special schools, though 'labelling' and assumptions about lack of achievement were still encountered and were hurtful:

But I was very hurt last year because I was in the pool with another teacher who hadn't seen him before in the water. She came up to me and said, 'Oh, doesn't he love the water.' And I said, 'Yes, he comes to life in the water.' She said, 'It amazes me how our non-achievers always love the water.'

I went home, I didn't really think she'd said it! You know you can't believe that someone would say something like that. But I went home and didn't stop crying for two days.

And yet he's achieved so much. He's not supposed to be able to walk, and he's walking. He takes his coat off. He knows when he comes in you have to unzip his coat and he can take it off. He'll take his balaclava off if you start him off.

Being Grateful

Some adult respondents also talked about particular good teachers who 'treated you like anybody else'. However, there was a more general experience (similar to my own) that a kindly patronisation is not conducive to high academic expectations, and one respondent summed up an aspect of this ethos by vivid reference to 'a culture of being grateful':

Well I feel that at school and college there was this definite culture of being grateful for the fact that they were looking after you. Because, obviously, when you are a kid, there's this parent role isn't there? I can only talk in hindsight. As you get older you think about it. There was definitely that culture. You can't say all members of staff, because some were fantastic. They treated you as an individual, but there was this general thing that basically they made you feel that 'If it weren't for us, where would you be?' And as I said to one of them once, who I didn't particularly like, 'If it weren't for us, what job would you be doing?'

The Need for Change

The interviewees were aware of particular positive and negative aspects of their schooling but they also had a more general awareness that, with transformed attitudes and more resources, it could have been so much more educative and pleasant:

Well, I think for it to really work it would have to be such a revolution of attitude. We'd have to really see people as individuals and cater for their individual range of needs, interests, abilities, disabilities, and part of the education of all of us would be much more about attitude and be value based. Moral education, personal, social education, all those things I think are so important, because it is all about the things that make people understand. Like in the year of the disabled, that big poster of a young man in a wheelchair – 'His biggest problem is you.' Now I just think all of that is so true. If we all had much more awareness of valuing people and seeing people as an individual and seeing them as a person first, and what their disabilities or abilities are second, and valuing everybody equally, regardless of their range of ability or disability, then my daughter and I would have had much less of the hurtful experiences we've talked about and she would have been stretched more, and had more of a curriculum that matched her, you know? ... But you know it's such an alternative society, and such an alternative education system that we're talking about.

Resources: The Need for More and Better School Resources

As we saw, the issue of resources emerged in relation to needs identified in the child's statement. The issue of resources in schools was also a general recurring theme in most of the interviews when respondents talked about their experiences of school:

I think he needs one to one but he gets nothing. I mean last term he used to have half an hour [of] occupational therapy on a Monday and she said she was getting a response from him. But he only had half an hour a week.

* * *

He's always loved outings but then he wasn't allowed to go on outings any more, because he has rectal Valium. And they are not allowed to go out unless there's anyone on the bus that can give rectal Valium, and they'd only got two teachers at the whole of the school that could give rectal Valium.

* * *

Well, I mean ideally the school would love to have a physio there every day, somebody there to give her physio every day, but with cutbacks and one thing and another, they only have a physio come in three times a week, but they have to train their own staff to do the physio with her.

* * *

The school did an equipment demonstration which we went to. They had some brilliant equipment to really help the severely disabled a lot. I'm sure the school would love to have equipment like that of their own but they just haven't you know. But you can't really blame the school 'cos they can't afford it.

* * *

There isn't enough speech therapy basically. I have fought this the whole of the way through both primary and secondary, actually, ever since one of the neurosurgeons wrote originally to her primary school to say that he was very concerned that she wasn't getting enough speech therapy on a regular basis. And I have really fought for it all the way through secondary school and still not got very far.

These concerns about levels of resources are widely shared. There is, for example, a concern amongst head teachers of mainstream schools, too, that general cuts in LEA budgets are affecting the levels of support that can be provided to pupils with special needs, thereby creating problems for the school. They believe that an increase in resources is required to meet the Code of Practice and the demands of the National Curriculum for pupils with learning difficulties (Derrington *et al.* 1996).

Integration

The Warnock Report (1978) proposed that most pupils currently in special schools should be integrated into ordinary schools, and this was given legal force by the Education Act 1981. Special schools would educate the smaller proportion of pupils with severe or complex disabilities and should strengthen their links with ordinary schools, offering short-term provision, providing specialist expertise and acting as resource centres. Since 'integration' was the term associated with Warnock, and was a familiar term used by our respondents, it is a term frequently used in this text. However, as was discussed in Chapter 1, perhaps in some ways a more useful term is 'inclusion'. 'Inclusion' as a concept perhaps more readily suggests that there can be, as discussed below, many supportive and flexible ways of ensuring that a particular child is not excluded from the mainstream, within an ethos where so-called 'special provision' is seen as part of the 'normal' requirements of a diverse student body. It could also be seen to incorporate the society beyond school too, in representing an ideal or goal to move towards; a society in which disabled people are no longer excluded or isolated in so many ways.

Within education, inclusion, with all its advantages, will only work, however, if the 'education for all' dimension of promoting equal opportunities is not neglected. All pupils in the school should develop a disability-aware perspective. The Warnock Report captured this wider need to change attitudes to 'the handicapped'. Integration/inclusion is thus a potential benefit in the moral education of all the school population.

There is strong advocacy for the inclusion of all children in ordinary schools, from advocacy groups such as the Centre for Studies in Integrated Education, the Integration Alliance and parent groups. They argue that children have a right to attend their ordinary, neighbourhood school. Nothing provided in special schools could not be provided in ordinary ones.

However, the Warnock Report points out that integration will only be effective if certain conditions are fulfilled. These conditions are that there should be planned entry, support by the governing body, a designated specialist teacher, a school-based resource centre and a planning framework by the LEA. In short, successful integration requires careful planning, adequate support and in-service training for the teachers. Supporting special needs training for more (ideally all) teachers should be a governor priority. In many primary schools, the designated teacher is a class teacher who is given insufficient time for this additional role.

A second NFER research project (Derrington *et al.* 1996), also conducted from summer 1995 to autumn 1996, investigated the position of pupils with special needs in the 1990s, with the aim of mapping the position regarding integration and examining the impact of recent education and resourcing strategies on the integration of pupils with special educational needs. The researchers looked at resourcing (amounts available and mechanisms for use), parental preference, attitude of schools and parents to inclusion, and the effect of the National Curriculum on schools' ability or willingness to provide appropriate support for the needs of all pupils. Overall the findings of the research match the experience of our respondents. For example, the research report concludes by emphasising the importance of the resource issue:

> The other main requirement for improving pupils' access to the curriculum is that sufficient resources are available to allow schools to employ appropriate numbers of learning support teachers and assistants so that both in-class support and individual tuition can be provided when required. In order to optimise the support provided by those staff, both they and their subject specialist colleagues need to have timetabled opportunities to collaborate both on the production of appropriate materials and to discuss the progress of pupils. (p. 128)

They also found, as did our respondents, that some teachers 'still hold the perception that the difficulties lie with the pupils rather than the interaction between the pupils and the school structures and environment'.

Schools were found to vary considerably in their attitude to, and resourcing of, pupils with special needs. Schools with larger proportions of such pupils have made more structural changes to support inclusion and spent more time discussing these issues with staff. The need for more professional training and support for teachers is emphasised, echoing our own emphasis on drawing out the education and training implications of the experiences of disabled pupils and students.

Integration (as inclusion) is a *process*, not a single event. 'Integration' may take various forms. It may involve social integration (e.g. lunchtime mixing, shared leisure facilities), locational integration (e.g. special units in mainstream schools) or functional integration (e.g. shared lessons and classes). Vaughan and Wertheimer (1989) argue that integration should take a form appropriate to each individual child, though geared to her or his eventual full integration into the mainstream:

> Integration can be developed in many different ways and it is, above all, a continuous process rather than a one-off placement. For one child it may involve being in an ordinary class full time, for another it may involve spending only part of each day or week with non disabled children. But ... full social and physical integration remains the ultimate goal and the process involved should be geared towards achieving this object. (p. 111)

For many children, then, a first stage should be planning, and a phased entry into the ordinary school. For some children, to stay in a special school but to attend ordinary school for social, and some educational, activities may be the best option. For other children, full phasing into the ordinary school may be the aim. Once in an ordinary school, children with special needs may be in one of a variety of kinds of special unit, or in an ordinary class and withdrawn for special small-group work, or given 'within class' support.

There are advantages to the 'within ordinary class' form of support, which is worthy of further development and monitoring. Withdrawal-group work should be planned in collaboration with the full-class teacher. In a school with a special unit, a member of the governing body should have a special concern for the unit. Special units are best attached to an ordinary school, rather than to some other kind of establishment, such as a child guidance centre.

The focus of Ann Lewis's (1995) book, *Children's Understanding of Disability*, is the issue of young people involved in *link projects*. These are projects in which children from special schools and from mainstream schools work together regularly over a number of years to develop integrated classes. For both groups of children, Lewis reports, the link project with which she was involved provided unique linguistic and social experiences and increased effective communication between non-disabled children and children with learning difficulties.

The projects embodied features associated with positive attitude change: structured and collaborative working and a positive ethos. They also increased the range of resources available to the children in both mainstream and special schools. The former gained access to specialist resources such as a soft playroom and multi-sensory environments and the latter could use a wider range of classroom resources.

Our parent respondent who is a special school teacher had experienced a link project both as a parent and as a teacher. She, too, had found it to be a positive experience:

> At school we actually do have interaction projects with mainstream secondary schools. And at first the girls and boys found it quite difficult to cope with somebody like my daughter who was quite a challenge for them to do things with. But they did actually find there was an awful lot of things they could do and they managed very well. So on both sides it worked very well. I think there are certain areas with certain youngsters where they could gain an awful lot from being in certain mainstream

lessons. I mean we have youngsters that are extremely good at art for instance, who would develop if they had the right tuition. So, maybe there are areas in which we could integrate an awful lot more. I think there is something to be said for having very much closer links than we have now. Our more vulnerable youngsters would have problems if they were in mainstream. There's a danger that if you are in a small unit on a mainstream school site, that you will not actually integrate as much as you do when you're separate but in a link project.

In the best possible world most disabled children could and would be successfully integrated into the mainstream, since the pupil and teacher attitudes and the institutional ethos, resources and structures they would encounter would facilitate their learning and welfare. This is not the best possible world but we could, in principle, improve it. In practice, however, we seem not to be moving in this direction. Although the National Curriculum emphasises the commonality of curriculum entitlement for all children, the Education Reform Act of 1988 was not, overall, conducive to integration. As Hegarty (1989) points out: 'The proposed educational reforms pose a particular challenge to special needs provision. If schools become more specialised and competitive, the traditional rationale for integrating education in terms of expanding comprehensive schooling will be less relevant. What price special needs when schools are driven by market forces?'

A Good Idea If ...

Most of the parents interviewed felt that 'integration' was good in principle but had reservations in practice. These reservations were about the attitudes of children and teachers in the mainstream, about the lack of adequate resources and about how secure an environment would be provided for their physically vulnerable children. Many subject teachers in the mainstream, like the parents, believe that integration is right in principle but requires adequate levels of resources to support disabled pupils and appropriate staff development to enable staff to teach them effectively.

Comments from parents included:

> In theory, integration into mainstream school is a brilliant idea. In practice, it couldn't work unless more money is put into the schools and the children

who have the needs are given the right facilities of a one-to-one teacher or a smaller class group. Put a child like mine into a class of 30 able-bodied children and he wouldn't survive. He'd be lost because he hasn't got the voice to fight; he hasn't got the ability to run around.

* * *

One of the things that happened to Sarah when she was at mainstream school, she never did anything without an ancillary, and as a result she wouldn't do anything without an ancillary, and when she went to the other school she wouldn't join in things because there was no adult with her and she had to regain that sort of confidence, so it has to be done absolutely correctly to work. But I would support it if it was done correctly and nicely. If it can't be done properly then I would rather it wasn't done at all, because by changing school Sarah is sometimes top of the class for something. If it can't be done properly it could be destructive, and people who make the rules and decisions aren't the people who've been destroyed, are they? It's the people they make the decision about who suffer the consequences of no support, no money, no this, no that, or of incorrectly put in support.

* * *

I know in certain countries they do an awful lot more integration than we do don't they? In the fact that they have classes within a secondary school that cater for youngsters who've got quite severe special needs. And I think if it was managed properly with enough resources, in great big letters, put into it, I think possibly it could work. It's one of these things that unless you tried it you wouldn't know, I think.

* * *

Well, she was never the top in the mainstream and that is soul destroying. When she first went to mainstream school, she didn't know what it was to be star girl. Not to be top in her school work but for someone to pick out something that meant she'd done well and that she deserved a reward for that! On the other hand I think it was quite useful for her to be with other children for at least a little while. They said that she pinched and poked and prodded and wouldn't wait in queues, but we never found that. And she did have a bit of pinching and pushing at this school too. People can move faster than she can so they do it to her and go. Whereas she gets caught because she is much slower. Integration depends very much on if the head teacher will have them. All the teachers kept saying, 'Oh, we haven't had anybody like this before. What do we do?' Well, most of us as parents haven't dealt with it before either but you have to get on with it. Nobody trained us in epilepsy or any other thing. They're only having to be teachers aren't they? They're trained to be a teacher! I find it very frustrating.

Since all of the parents we interviewed had concerns about his or her child coping in an (unchanged) mainstream school, we should note here that there is some evidence (Hall 1997) that up to 36 per cent of parents with a child in a special school wanted a change of school, mostly to a mainstream one.

Many of the adults we interviewed were also ambivalent about special education and about the special education they themselves had received, because special schools increase marginalisation. They do not promote social inclusion.

> Well it was a special school for disabled people so that I feel it cut me off from society, from normal society because I was mixed in with children that had disabilities, so I never had the experience with people who didn't have disabilities.

* * *

> Looking back there should have been more integration at an earlier age, not just for my benefit but for everyone's benefit. I think too it would have been a massive culture shock if I had gone straight from school to university … more integration earlier would have been, perhaps, useful.

Of course, these adult respondents had been educated at school some time ago (though most were young adults). However, recent research indicates that, even in the 1990s, attitudes to integration remain problematic in the mainstream. Barriers to increased integration were perceived by LEAs as including unfavourable attitudes by parents and teachers in both special and mainstream schools (NFER 1996).

The single most often expressed point of view about the integration (inclusion) of disabled children was that it would be extremely educative for mainstream society:

I think integration is fantastic, very important. It's good for both sides. The children in the mainstream school can learn from them and vice versa. The children from the mainstream school can learn to accept these children as normal children and not be afraid of them. And they'll grow up hopefully realising that. They'll be educated! These children aren't to be feared and have the right to be in society and they have a lot to offer as well. The mainstream children can see this for themselves and I'm certain that there are a lot of adults that need educating because they don't really understand.

* * *

The thing about integration of schools, if the children are taught from when they are little, ordinary children mixed with the special needs, they'd grow up with these children and learn to accept them. Whereas, if they've never been shown, you know, if they never see these children, they are a bit frightened and they are cruel as well.

* * *

I think as long as the disabled children have the right sort of help, integration is the best thing possible, because it's the only way that disability is ever going to be accepted, if it's there all the time. A lot of PH [physically handicapped] students have a perfectly normal brain. I don't think there is a case for them to be in a special school if they are physically healthy to take the normal roughs and smooths. I'm not so sure about our youngsters getting a fair crack of the whip. I think you've got to educate the outside world.

* * *

I was against integrating my child in case she got hurt but I do think that if kids know somebody they just accept that person. It's like myself when I first started working with the elderly. I thought, 'these poor people, not being able to do anything'. That's the way I saw them when I first started. But after a while I thought, 'Gosh, these people are amazing when you realise what age they [are] and what they [are] actually doing. And it was 'there's Sarah, there's Mollie'. It wasn't 'them old people' anymore. It was 'Mollie' and 'Sarah' because you know them. So, I suppose it could be the same for integration. The mainstream children accept them for who they are instead of what they think they are.

The disabled adult interviewees mentioned 'integration' less frequently, but expressed similar views about its educative aspect:

> Mainstream children would learn. They would learn and it would stop all this 'spastic' bit. 'Oh look at that big kid in that chair.' You know, showing off with their mates. I think they'd get that understanding … not ridicule. I do really think that.

★ ★ ★

> I definitely agree with integration. I think that it would open people's eyes and give them a new outlook into that sort of thing. At the moment, because disabled children and disabled adults are put into, made to go to special schools, instead of being mixed, a special group instead of being mixed with 'normal' people, that's why 'normal' people have got their attitude towards us. Definitely.

★ ★ ★

> I think that integration is a wonderful idea. I think it is a very positive thing. When I was a child you didn't get to see people with disabilities. They went away to their schools or their institutions, and so people of my generation and older are frightened unless you have got somebody in the family. If you get them integrated at a younger age and they grow up as part of the norm, you're going to lose the prejudice about that person, so you're not going to shy away. It's down to education, if you educate people at an early age, the older they get, the better they are going to be able to cope with things.

Although our respondents discussed the beneficial impact of being educated alongside disabled children on the 'mainstream' children, there is evidence that the attitude of mainstream teachers will also be affected. In discussing why, despite the moral imperative for inclusive schools and the empirical evidence in their favour, inclusion has progressed so slowly, Thomas, Walker and Webb (1998) point to 'fear of the unknown'. The inclusion project analysed in their comprehensive book on the subject shows that 'schools can successfully change to include children with even serious disabilities' and that many mainstream staff who were highly sceptical of the project before it started 'changed their views entirely after several months of seeing it in practice and were fulsome in their support for inclusion' (Thomas *et al.* 1998, p.118).

The Schooling Experience: Some Tentative Conclusions

As one would expect, the endemic prejudices about disability and the problems about resources for disabled people, illustrated in Chapter 2, also impact within education. Prejudice in pupils is still a factor which hinders integration/inclusion and, sadly, infects some teachers, even well-meaning teachers, in both sectors. Problems about resources also occur in both special and mainstream schools.

About the particular issue of statementing we found two sides of the coin. On the positive side, parents had appreciated their own involvement in the process, but in terms of the needs identified we found a particularly significant example of the resources problem. Schools simply were not adequately resourced to meet identified educational needs. Also, parents were not clear about the fact that an annual review of needs is supposed to take place.

There are different professional views about the merits or otherwise of statementing. What is perhaps clearer, both to professionals and to the parents who stressed the unique combination of the needs of their child, is that the schooling process must recognise this wide range of abilities, disabilities and learning needs of pupils who each combine these in a unique way. This should be reflected in an emphasis on a corresponding 'differentiation' in the curriculum. Good practice recognises the importance of differentiating tasks, materials and teaching styles according to the differing needs of the pupils in the class.

About the particular issue of 'integration', the inclusion of disabled children in mainstream education, three strong points emerged:

1. For integration/inclusion to work well, mainstream schools need to change to become more aware of prejudiced assumptions about disability, to be better resourced and to be more secure for particularly vulnerable children.

2. Partial inclusion, particularly in well-planned link schemes, seems to have been a positive experience on all sides.

3. There was strong agreement among respondents with the principle of inclusion. It was argued that if inclusion was well planned and

resourced from the perspective of the well-being of disabled children, this would have huge educational benefits for *all* children.

This conclusion chimes with research on integration which suggests that improved learning for mainstream children could also be an outcome of inclusion. Thus the NFER review of research on this issue suggested:

> From an initial concern with particular aspects of integrating pupils with special needs, research focus has moved on to the ways in which ordinary schools have to change in order to accommodate pupils with special needs. The deeper understanding of the interactive nature of learning difficulties and how schools can prevent them, that flowed from this, has benefited both pupils with special needs and many others not usually regarded as the concern of special education. (Hegarty 1989, p.111)

In particular, integration could contribute to personal, social and moral education. Ann Shearer (1981) has put this succinctly and well:

> It will offer them a chance to learn a lesson that is often now denied them: that the world in which they live is made up of people with a variety of abilities and inabilities and that that variety is a large one. It will offer them a perspective in which to live with the quota of abilities and inabilities that is their own – a perspective that is based on tolerance of difference, rather than its rejection. And in the arrangements that are made to meet the individual needs of children who have been defined as 'special' they could find the space to explore those of their own needs that are special too. Then schools could be on the way to becoming real places of learning and growth – for all children. (p.150)

In the long term, inclusion would make a significant contribution to countering the endemic prejudices against the disabled, currently socially entrenched and affecting the day-to-day lives of disabled people.

CHAPTER 4

Post-School Education and Training
'A Long Way to Go'

Our respondents' experiences of post-school education and training can, as in the previous chapter, be conveniently grouped into three key aspects: experiences of post-school further and higher education; preparation for employment (careers advice and training); and the idea of a continuing education for differently abled people, with a disability-aware perspective for all. As with schooling, prejudiced attitudes and inadequate resources (including lack of information) proved to be significant in post-school educational experience. (The problem about information may have been partially alleviated by the requirement of the Disability Act 1995 that further and higher educational institutions provide information about their facilities for disabled people.)

Our adult respondents had, between them, experience of both further and higher education. Our parent respondents, whose children were mostly at the schooling phase of education, expressed anxieties about their children's futures.

Preparation for employment was, as we shall see, unsatisfactory, with inadequate vocational preparation and advice at school, and limited training opportunities. In terms of employment, the prejudices and discrimination of a 'disablist' society tend to mean either difficult or menial employment situations on the one hand, or the social isolation of unemployment on the other.

The general picture could be characterised as having worsened in that once schooling is at an end, there are inadequate opportunities for the lifelong learning of disabled people, insufficient disability-aware education for professionals, parents and the public at large, and worsening social attitudes to disabled individuals. Although most of our adult respondents were in further or higher education or in professional careers, in national terms the employment prospects for disabled people are bleak.

Our respondents believed that they had had to prove themselves, and had to be better than their non-impaired colleagues in order to succeed. Their undoubted achievements had been obtained by determination in the face of additional hurdles and barriers.

Experience of Post-School Education

Further Education

This young woman had, in the recent past, made the transition from schooling to further education and had felt this to be a disempowering experience, with too little reference to her own wishes and decisions:

> I mean basically, I didn't have any useful careers advice and the advice I did have, I personally didn't have a say. My careers officers had a say, my parents had a say, but not me. And the only time that I ever found out about things was when people used to turn up on my doorstep and say, 'This is the next step for you.' And I used to say, 'Well who decided it? I didn't. I haven't even had a say. I'm virtually an adult and you're still walking over me.' You see, because I'd been let down in the past, I always used to think that I'd be let down again. And I always used to say to my parents, 'Well if I'm to go away or if I'm to do something that's different, please let me go up and suss the situation out first myself, because I'll be able to know best whether I'll be happy there.'

* * *

> The thing was, you see, people never used to listen. I mean I went to one place, for an interview, and I sussed it out and all it was was a special school for mentally handicapped children under the age of ten. I would have been the oldest person in the school there if I had gone and there was one mobile and one typewriter and one typing teacher and that was it! And I said to my father, 'Well, that's not for me because I'm not mentally handicapped.' My choice would have been to go to a college of my choice where I would have been happy or maybe just left school and found a job with a firm that I was really happy with. That would have been my choice. Instead of that I think I did about six, seven years' extra education, which I mean is a lot really, especially if you don't get what you want. So I said to my father, 'Well, in

fairness to me, I've done everything everybody else wants me to do, and I have passed. I've got all the grades and things that I should have got but it would be nice for me now if I could just be me and people started treating me as an adult, and they realised that I'm leading my life for me, and that they can't just walk over me.'

Another respondent, who had recently attended a residential special college, had also experienced this lack of recognition of her adult status: 'I liked the college but my only negative feeling towards that was, ... the way we were treated by the staff ... we were told before we actually went there we would be treated like adults.'

Similarly,

We were told we could have baths when we wanted to and then the situation suddenly changed and they said, 'Oh no, you've got to have a bath tonight.' And we said, 'Why?' And then they said, 'Well, you've got to have your name put down in this book.' And we said, 'But why?' And they wouldn't give us a reason and they kept badgering us to put our names in this book, you see, and they said that's the correct procedure. Whereas I felt that college should have been for *not* trying to get the students to do what they didn't want to do because the aim of that college was to make the students as independent as possible – do their own washing and that sort of thing, their own ironing ... so they've got some sort of experience for when they actually go out into the world.

Another told us of a friend who, upon leaving college,

They've just bundled her off into an old people's home. There is nobody of her own age there for her to talk to or go out with and enjoy herself and have a social life, which she hasn't got at all. She's stuck there day in, day out and got nothing to do.

This student attends a mainstream college of further education:

Some students need excuses and exaggerate their illness and I always tried not to be off sick unless I was absolutely really lousy. With my condition I have a memory problem so I have to write everything down. It's the only way I can jog my memory. So you know that kind of help wasn't there. I always had it extra hard. To prove myself I was always a hard worker. I was always the one that was in the library at 9.30 every day and didn't leave until it closed at 10.00 p.m.

Higher Education

Another student, this time in higher education, echoed this experience of a lack of procedure for meeting different or additional needs, making the additional point that it should not be the responsibility of an individual student to make demands in a situation without adequate institutional procedures.

'... but there is no policy for disability so it is always put upon the individual. So you can start to feel that you are just somebody who is always demanding.' 'It is always put on to you to say what you need.'

Physical access issues are still a problem in some institutions!

The toilets were half-way through floors; you could get a lift to the floor you wanted but the toilets were half-way through. Do you know what I mean? Between the levels. That was never solved. It was raised. There was always this argument that there is a toilet on the ground floor, but we were always on the fourth floor, you know? It was the same with the coffee machine. There was a huge debate once about the fire situation, because they had a fire alarm practice and you are not supposed to use the lifts in that situation ... I can go down certain steps, but that is not the point, some people can't. Some people in a wheelchair, what can they do?

★ ★ ★

A couple of weeks back I had a fall in the university. The ladies' toilet I went to has two steps. There were warning signs on the door but the door was wedged and the warning sign was on the other side so I just walked through and there were two steps and I fell over on my knees. I hurt my knees. There [were] no white lines on the steps. The excuse they gave me was the warning sign was on the door but the door was wide open!

There was also evidence of a lack of preparation for the independent study required in higher education:

I doubt whether the blind students I have met have been sufficiently coached and prepared for professional life, you know? And this again is a little niggle at the back of my mind. I sometimes feel that the blind students

I meet who are in the sixth forms preparing for university entrance (occasionally I get contacts from them or their parents), I often wonder whether their study techniques are really up to the way they have got to be to survive. I don't know anything about how they are trained but I often find they don't know much. For example, the use of cassettes is very unsophisticated. They have no understanding of four tracked, half speed cassette recording machines, although in my opinion that is the only way a blind student can effectively manage who is using the cassette mode. So I am not sure that things are as good as they should be among those students.

Educational Resources

The problematic issue of inadequate resources for disabled people identified at the outset as a feature of our society and clearly seen in the context of schooling, was also a significant factor in further and higher educational institutions:

There are so many unmet needs which I don't think will ever be met ... I mean the lecturers could give me a large copy of the lecture notes, even give it to me in advance. 'This is the lecture for next week.' Then I could get prepared and take part in the discussion going on. But you don't get that. Last year when I first started I used to go and ask lecturers, 'Can I have large print copies?' But I never got it so in the end you just give up. You're fighting and you lose out on the energy. You make do.

* * *

Before I started my course in September, I went to see the administrator in July and did say to her, 'Look, I want to go and do this course, but these are my problems ...' 'Oh you shouldn't have problems. We've had students in the past who are blind and who did the course so you shouldn't have any problems.' But they didn't realise that students who had done the course before were blind from birth or early years so when they started university they were all prepared for it.

* * *

I needed more support. So after starting the course when everybody was getting on with their work, I was running around like mad because I couldn't cope with it, because I couldn't see what the lecturers were writing on the board and when I was taking notes, I couldn't read my own notes, and this added to my stress.

One academic made an important distinction between helpfulness to and from an individual, on the one hand, and institutional structures of support on the other:

I wanted this university to adopt as a policy principle that any additional costs which might arise through having a disabled academic would be met centrally by the university rather than falling on the particular unit or skill where the disabled academic was working, because it seemed to me that that would enhance the dignity of the academics and prevent one feeling that one was a liability upon one's immediate colleagues. I was never able to get the university to accept that principle, not that it was ever turned down either. I think it was one of those which fell between the cracks, maybe one or two acknowledged the question. Having said that, I always found that whenever I needed anything, I got it. If I wanted four or five more APH reading machines, I got them. In that respect they were wonderful to me. But on the principles, I think they found it difficult because they were always concerned about what those principles might lead to, and so it was, I think, a case of individual understanding but not principled support from the institution. I bet that's typical.

This student makes an excellent point about provision for new needs:

I started with a magnifying glass which wasn't much good, went to the desk and I said, 'Have you got something like CC TV that I can use to read this book?' She said, 'We've got things for hearing impairment but not visual impairment because nobody has asked about it and if you go downstairs and ask our senior librarian he might have something to offer.' So I went down and wasted about a couple of hours and they couldn't find anything, and I said I would call it a day and come another day. That's the sort of response you get. I know it's hard for normal people to realise that every disability is different but there should be some provision for meeting new needs.

The 'Catch 22' identified in Chapter 2, that even where resources exist, lack of information about them can be a significant problem, is graphically illustrated in the higher education context. This person, in spite of his own initiative in approaching the university in advance, received this information very late, after experiencing many difficulties, and then only through a previous student and a sympathetic blind lecturer:

> And I didn't know what equipment was available to me. I only found out when I spoke to a senior lecturer. This other student did the course and he gave me the number of the lecturer. He was blind and when he walked in I thought be would be walking with a white stick but he was walking like a normal person. I sat talking to him and then he said, 'You don't have to use the white stick if you can get your way round. I've got my stick, I keep it in my pocket. I use it for crossing the road and when there is danger.' He said, 'Hasn't the university done anything for you?' and I said 'No'. He said, 'Look, everything should have been set up for you in the holiday. You should have a specialist computer and you should have readers and personal support and you can get an extra grant for all that.' Now all these things I didn't know. These facilities were all available and I would have applied for all those.

A woman with a condition predisposing her to fatigue and illness had these experiences in doing her PhD:

> It is just very very difficult to convey my condition to somebody who has normal health. Ironically, one of my supervisors who actually has always described herself as fit, said, 'Well, I have exactly that,' and you kind of feel that your experiences are being belittled. You know it's like when you are doing a PhD within four years and you know, forget about being ill, you still have to finish within four years. My doctor said not to spend long periods of time in front of a computer. That became a real problem for me for doing the work. My supervisor did approach the director of the department to get some secretarial help and he never really got it off the ground, because I don't think they care or understand.

One student had studied for a first degree in Education and complained about the Education campus. Little was done to improve matters. When she wanted, subsequently, to go on to do her post-graduate Certificate of Education:

What was quite nasty was that Education didn't want to have me. They actually put up all sorts of arguments and when the chips were down they made it academic. It was only the sociology department [where she had also studied] going back to them and saying, 'Look, this is a load of rubbish.' I always feel that they took me under sufferance and they didn't want me in. The teaching profession does not want disabled people basically.

There had also been positive experiences of further and higher education but, sadly, less of these:

My impairment progressed and by the end of school I was finding walking to the classrooms difficult. The school experience, on the whole, was not a good one. Children can be very cruel. Mainstream school experience wasn't a good one for that reason. Calling me names. I mean everybody has that at school but, obviously, if you stand out from them all it's going to be that much more. College experience was better. It matched the culture of 'learning organisation' that colleges are. Students are there because they want to be there. They're not being forced to be there. And looking at the more practical things, at college they were keen to be helpful. They would organise a class session in a room that was nearer.

* * *

It was total integration in the university. It was like automatic adjustment. There was no culture shock involved and because I lived in residential, they had care staff there. At university it was the first time I had used community service volunteers for myself and I had two volunteers always throughout my time at university.

One university student gave a picture of slowly improving facilities with many improvements achieved but still 'a long way to go':

Well, we have here facilities I suppose comparable to other universities, whether they are any better or not I don't really know. We have a tutor for disabled students who is available, I think it's, let me see, I think she's supposed to be available ten hours a week ... She's a lecturer on our academic staff but she serves this university-wide function. It is not a full-time post. It's not even a half-time post, I think it's 10 or 12 hours a week. It should perhaps be extended a bit but she does a very useful job. There are procedures for her to give advice on all applicants who express on their application form some disablement. She interviews them and advises departments on their participation. Let's see, we are just creating a mobility map of the campus under [the] terms of the HEFC (Higher Education Funding Council) funding for schemes to increase access. We're also creating at the present time a carved wooden model of the campus for blind students which will have acoustics built into it so that you will touch a relevant building and you'll get on a cordless headset, the acoustic ambience of that building. We expect to have this finished and up and running in September. It's being made right now, that will be a wonderful facility for blind students. Let's see, in the main library we have a resource centre for handicapped students which was formally opened earlier this term. It contains quite a wide variety of equipment including 'reading edge', the computer-driven reading machine; there is one of those over there. There's another 'reading edge' in the education library for [the] use of blind students using the school of education. That's all happened in the past 12 months since that equipment became available. I'm not quite sure what facilities are like for students with hearing impairment. I know there are a number of such students on campus. The physical access and mobility of our campus is very mixed. Some of the older buildings are quite difficult. New buildings are adapted, not always terribly efficiently and there is a rolling programme of continual adaptation. For example, the foyer of this building has recently had a wheelchair lift installed to enable people to get up from the lower concourse to the concourse where the lift was. So we've recently had that installed. Clearly we have a long way to go.

Prejudice in Education

Like schools, institutions of further and higher education reflect those endemic negative attitudes and prejudices of the society of which they are a part; the attitudes identified in Arena 2 in Chapter 2 were as pervasive in post-school education as elsewhere:

> People talked about my friend's personal condition, which involved private stuff about his body, in front of people. I mean it's that sort of thing which is just insensitive.

* * *

They had meetings every morning, and I know this because I became a very good friend with one of the care staff there who attended these meetings. He said it was just outrageous. They would say things like, 'S's going out with R now. We've got to keep an eye on that.' To that level! What is that about, you know? I hated things like that.

* * *

We need help and we need support but we don't need vigilising, which you get a lot of the time. Instead of treating us as a human being, or individual, we get 'poor such and such'. We don't want sympathy, we want help. It's hard to get it, you know, just the one and not the other.

Careers Advice, Training and Employment
Careers Advice and Training

We uncovered a picture of inadequate careers advice and preparation, with poor subsequent training. Youth training schemes were experienced by a small number of our respondents, and these had not proved useful, providing little in terms of either skills or employment.

A parent:

The Youth Training Schemes aren't geared up very well enough for disabled young people. Mainstream training provision gave her nothing except an experience in failure.

A trainee:

I've found voluntary work more acceptable and I'm more at ease now than I ever was on any placement doing anything, and I feel I get more out of voluntary work than I did when I was on both the training schemes because I'm free to be left to do what I want to do, but under such supervision that I'm not made to feel nervous or tense all the time, thinking or feeling that I've done something wrong.

And I'm also being accepted for who I am and not because I'm disabled which is also something I like. It's something that makes a lot of difference if you're accepted for who you are and not because you've got a disability ... with some people its 'oh look, that girl's got such and such wrong with her, let's make fun of her', that sort of ... thing, whereas at the Guide Dogs for the Blind I don't get that. I might have a disability but it doesn't bother me and they just help me if I can't do anything, can't do whatever it is that they've given me to do because I find it a little bit difficult, and they give me a bit of help then you see, but they just accept me for who I am.

A teacher of up-coming school leavers:

We have what they call 'leavers' review', which is like an annual review that is done with a view to what we would like for them in the future. But what we would like and what we're likely to get [are] totally different I think. They don't get [a] chance to talk to anybody very much before they actually decide where they are going to go. Provision is very poor at the moment because of course there have been a lot of cuts, and the fact that they closed workshops.

Some of our youngsters actually get college placements with special needs courses. That lasts for either a year or two years and it's for a day, sometimes less, a week, and they get no provision any other time. Well, the youngsters that have that are not actually very likely to be employed on a paying basis really. Some of them do go on work experience and come across things that they are very good in, nursery classes, playgroups, things like that. They are a very good help because they are nice with the youngsters, which little three/four-year-olds love. I mean they love an older girl or boy to actually do things with them like that, some are very good in that school. But of course, they would never be able to actually do any training because they wouldn't be able to cope with the written, academic side of it. So that causes problems.

An adult respondent, now in a professional career, felt that disabled people are treated as a commodity to fill day centres: 'My city had got a new day centre. Career training was geared towards that. They wanted to fill it. It was warehousing.'

Employment

Our respondents, as you would expect with any group of workers, had experienced a mixture of positive and negative working environments, colleagues and incidents.

A distinguished academic, for example, told us:

> I should say my own career has been very good since I lost my sight. You see I was already a senior lecturer; six years after I lost my sight I was promoted to a readership you see; another three years later I was given a personal chair; and the year after that I was appointed to be dean of this whole faculty, which put me on the senior management scale of the university. So actually I have found that the university has promoted me, you know, it's not hindered me in any way and in certain respects I suppose my academic output has been better since I lost my sight because of the concentration and careful planning which disability requires. Certainly when I was appointed dean I have been told that there were one or two eyebrows raised and people did say, as people will say, 'How will he manage? How will he cope with the paperwork?' People tend to say these things simply because they don't know how you do it. But on the other hand people generally assumed that I would manage and I think on the whole I did. I was never patronised in any way. I made it clear, for example, that I could not cope with papers tabled at meetings and the university were extremely good and I was always informed if there were going to be papers tabled at the meeting, they would be sent across to me; even an hour before the meeting I would get a phone call and somebody would be running across with a paper that was going to be tabled which would just give me an opportunity to read it before I went. So all of that I think worked quite well.

This contrasts with a disabled social worker who had found a more negative culture:

> I talked to another social worker and she actually said that the trouble with the profession is that they were always in the role of helper, and people with disabilities are expected to be the clients and not the people who were providing support.

PROVING ONESELF

What was striking was the number of respondents who felt they had to prove themselves against a climate of negative attitudes, assumptions and expectations – both in interviews and on first starting a new job:

Until you go to an interview, you don't know how switched on an employer will be. Some of the questions can be totally outrageous. Women have that too with 'You're gonna get married, you're gonna have children'.

★ ★ ★

I remember the first night I just didn't want to go but I went and I ... they were very nice and stuff but they were obviously very very wary and probably thought 'what the hell have we got here?' and I remember then just getting this menial thing to do. Then there was a bug going round and I think a lot of people caught it and they were very very short staffed and I just said 'I'll do it', and they realised I was capable of a lot more than they thought I was. And that was down to my disability, what I looked like and stuff, I'm sure it was, and within four weeks I had the same amount of responsibilities as the people that worked there all the time. I wasn't getting paid for it, but I worked overtime for them, and I was very committed ... In the end they were sorry to lose me, I think, and they said, 'When you finish your degree, come back and we'll find something.' I didn't really want to, but I think the reason I did this is because I didn't want to go home. You know, once you've lived away from home and you've got your independence you don't go back, especially if you require help.

★ ★ ★

I think you actually end up working much harder than your normal average worker because you are going to great lengths to prove yourself.

★ ★ ★

I fear that the big bad world outside is a tough world and it's very competitive, and a lot of potential employers aren't as switched on to the potential and the resource and the skill that a disabled person can bring to a company or an organisation. So, inevitably, if one's disabled, one's got to get over that, so you've got to perform that much better in an interview situation or filling in an application form, which is the first step.

★ ★ ★

Then I got the job of President of the Students' Union, an elected post which was good because I knew a lot of the people there anyway and they knew me. They were apprehensive; they said to me before I left that they thought, 'Oh my God, he's not going to be able to cope with the pressure, and he's always going to be off sick.' But I was the only member of staff not to have a day off that year and I was the only one to work 70–80 hours a week. So that went down really well and from that the post I'm in now came up and I applied and I got it again, and that's good because I'm still working in an environment in which people know me and I haven't had to start all over again.

* * *

I mean it's always like you have to work doubly hard to prove yourself.

There was also some tendency to pigeon-hole disabled people into work related to disability. There is a world of difference between *recognising* the contribution individuals can make arising from their own experience of impairment and *restricting* individual choices and opportunities to this field of work.

> What I have had a lot of is, 'Why don't you work with disabled children or disabled people?' I love being a generic social worker. I didn't want to be seen as a specialist in disability. I didn't want my boss to give me all the cases that had disability, and you have to be careful about that. A lot of colleagues would ask me if they had a case involving somebody with a disability. They would ask me questions and I don't mind helping them but I used to sometimes say, 'You could ask the person themselves that question.'

There was some evidence of a lack of meaningful occupational opportunities for the small number of our adult respondents who did not have formal qualifications from college or university:

> I went to a college for disabled youth. I liked the college but my only negative feeling was that we were treated like two-year-olds. After I left college I went on these two training schemes. I don't feel that I had the right sort of training for what I wanted to do. I don't feel I was listened to. I wasn't given enough time in any of the placements and was moved on quickly, without explanation. When I left [the] YTS [Youth Training Scheme] I was asked by this woman what I wanted to do and I said 'I really like children and I really like animals so I would like to work with children

or animals.' I was given the option of cleaning out toilets in a school or making up Christmas stockings for cats. Then a person who works for the Shaw Trust put me in touch with Guide Dogs for the Blind. I enjoy working with the dogs and actually seeing them placed with some of the blind people. It is voluntary work and I love it. I get much more out of it than when I was on the training schemes. I'm not made to feel nervous or tense all the time, thinking or feeling that I've done something wrong.

Several respondents commented that more flexible working conditions, such as decent part-time work and flexi-time, would be extremely valuable to some disabled employees. The medical condition of some impaired individuals may be associated with tiredness, occasional illness or frequent medical appointments. Clearly these conditions are much better accommodated by a working week that is not 8.30 a.m to 5.30 p.m. (or later), five days per week, the rigid pattern experienced by many employees.

HALF-HEARTED GESTURES

Access and the physical condition of many places of employment are still problems for many disabled employees:

> They do things for the disabled only half-heartedly. They do it so they can say, 'Oh we have done this for the disabled', but they are not helping the disabled. They hinder them, if anything, by only making things half safe, like wheelchair access or whatever.

* * *

> It's about *ad hoc* arrangements for individual workers. You know, the disabled toilet is always in the client area. There are social services offices built in the 80s which do not have wheelchair access to staff areas; they have wheelchair access to client areas, which actually speaks volumes, I think.

The children of our parent respondents were still at school and mostly too young to have experienced direct careers advice and training. Already, however, worries and concerns about their children's futures were shared by the parents:

> I do worry a lot actually because of the situation in C, where a lot of resources have been taken away and there are not many facilities. It does

worry me about his future … I'm hoping it will be more adequate by the
time he is older.

* * *

It frightens me to think that things are being closed down with nothing
left. Parents need something positive for their children to go to. I mean, I
wouldn't want to sit in a room all day long watching telly, whereas I would
like to go out and be able to occupy myself, stretch myself, maybe going to
a centre. You might only be mixing bolts and putting them in boxes, but
you would be socialising. You'd have a radio on, you'd be meeting people
and there would be a social life there. Whereas, if you are left alone, you
may as well be in prison because you don't get a social life.

* * *

I worry about when I'm no longer gonna be around, because I could
imagine that she could get to be quite isolated if things don't work out with
employment, you know?

One young woman who was older, 18 and coming up to school leaving, had
received no preparation and her mother was anxious that there seemed to be
no prospects for her continuing education or occupation:

I don't want education to stop at 19. Some of the youngsters get nearly an
extra year you see but her birthday's July and that's when the cut-off
comes. But having said that I do think she's ready to leave school. It's just a
worry as to what is going to happen because we don't really know, and it's
now the middle of March almost, and they leave in July and we don't know,
haven't heard a dicky bird about what's happening.

It happens that our adult respondents were mainly either in further/higher
education or employment, but in the small number of cases of unemployment, this concern about the social isolation of unemployment was
endorsed. The one parent whose adult daughter had already left school and
college felt there was yet another 'Catch 22'. Sometimes disabled people
have to accept boring and menial work below their capacities or face the
social isolation of unemployment:

She had her assessment at the assessment place and the only thing they
could come up with was that she should go to the day centre and do this

packing animal stockings, very mechanical, or cleaning. She turned that down. She said, 'No, I don't want to do either of those things, they sound boring.' And I thought that was good because I thought, 'Why should she get locked into something really boring, like cleaning or packing?' But of course the down side of that, by not having any work, though she's extremely good at finding things to do and keeping interested, she doesn't meet many people of her own age. Even there she does well, keeping up friendships from college and meeting people one way or another. But it's all down to her and there's big gaps where she's not really got enough people of her own age around and activities going on.

Lifelong Education For All

An enabling education would provide both flexible opportunities for the lifelong education of all people, including those with disabilities, and a disability-aware education for everyone.

More Flexible Provision

Our interviewees pointed to the need for a much more flexible provision of education, training and employment opportunities for disabled people, and the need for practical help that would make such opportunities real:

> I'm no lecturer, but I would say just for the students themselves to be able to achieve the best that they can, one needs to ensure that their needs are catered for, their practical needs.

In a world that caters for the 'averagely' abled, one's unique pattern of abilities and disabilities needs careful assessment so that it can be matched with appropriate and flexible training and employment. Without this kind of matching, which seems currently inadequate and under-resourced, difficulties become inevitable. This happened in a series of placements for one individual:

> I couldn't manage the till in the shop because of my number problems. My physical stature made lifting or carrying in the day centre for elderly people very difficult. I did very well on my placement on a switchboard except that when they were all ringing at once, I got very panicked and couldn't cope with it.

One parent interviewed pointed out that people with learning difficulties need more, not less, continuing education. Her daughter was at an age to leave school and ready to do so but needed more time for learning, at some kind of *bridging college*, before employment: 'I would prefer her really to have like a bridging period from school to training. I think many are still learning. I think they need education until they are well into their 20s, but she's getting past the age for school.'

An adult respondent also felt that, given that schooling seemed often to fail to stretch disabled pupils, there was an additional need for the kind of 'second chance' educational opportunities which adult education often represents:

> I did Pitman's English Stage One and got a pass and that's all I did at school. We didn't do exams. It wasn't expected. Since I married I worked and got my GCE English Language. I couldn't cope with literature because I haven't learned how to study. I can't read a book and dissect it and criticise. I wasn't taught to learn if that makes sense, so I feel that had I been in a different environment I would have achieved a lot more.

Disability Awareness

As we saw in Chapter 3, our respondents agreed that the greater inclusion of disabled children into mainstream education would have benefited mainstream children – in helping them to acquire greater knowledge and understanding about impairment and in countering endemic prejudices against the disabled. Many of them also expressed similar views about adulthood and the need for a disability-aware *continuing* education. Thus several people pointed out that prejudices are learned and thus need unlearning, sometimes in adulthood. 'Very young children have not got a problem, and I think it's adults that put the prejudices into them and I think that happens with colour and with disability as well.'

A parent: 'Much to my shame, I can't converse with an adult handicapped person. I can cope with my son and children that go to his school but with teenagers I feel very shy. And that's bad. I've got to get over that one and learn how to communicate with adults as well.'

Our respondents were aware not only of the prejudiced assumptions they had themselves met with in their daily lives, but also of the kind of general attitudes and stereotypes endemic in the general population:

> If you don't know a group you tend to just go by what you see on the telly. I mean, you see a disabled lad or girl on the telly, or an adult really, and you don't know that person and yet you think, 'That poor little person.' That's the way you think.

★ ★ ★

> There should be disability awareness across the board. Because if you are not brought up with awareness when you are young, you are going to have a prejudice when you are older.

★ ★ ★

> You read about dreadful things about holiday makers complaining about disabled children on the beach but apart from those very unpleasant people most people are kindly disposed, even if it's in a slightly patronising mode, to disabled children. They want to give them holidays and raise money and buy presents and all this. But it's as people get older that I think less allowances are made and less kindness is shown and more isolation can take place, and being cut out of things and not being regarded as being of value and people being embarrassed if there's anything different and looking away and all that sort of thing. So I think attitudes get worse actually as you get older.

★ ★ ★

> That sort of prejudice is there all the time. I mean you get this business of 'mentally handicapped' and 'mentally ill'. They can't see that there's a big difference; I don't know what you do. I think you need more courses and things but if people aren't interested they're not going to go anyway, are they? I think when I was working … I was thought of as 'Poor bugger, he's disabled, can't perform as well as anybody else.' It was never said to me, but I got that underlying feeling. For example, there was one particular woman there (I'll always remember it, probably until I die). The first time that she met me she could barely communicate with me. She'd never come up against disabled people before and it really threw her. She just couldn't relate. This was a highly educated woman. At that time the company only

employed graduates. She was completely spaced out. So you see, it was her problem. It wasn't my problem. Part of her education in life was lacking. And she had to have a steep learning curve. And to an extent one could say that permeated throughout the company because they didn't have disabled people working there, apart from me.

As was discussed in Chapter 1, this disability awareness needs to be incorporated into continuing professional education which would then perhaps be more likely to help the professionals recognise how much their disabled client or patient has learned from experience, to communicate better with them and to provide the best possible service. The curriculum implications are extensive. A disability-aware curriculum for professionals would need to be reoriented and extended in many ways. One professional respondent, for example, said that in all his training on courses about disability, sexuality was never addressed. There was perhaps an embarrassment, and an assumption that 'disabled people are asexual'.

Perhaps we should complete this section on the need for a disability-aware (school and post-school) education with a narrative which incorporates an incident of chillingly extreme prejudice. A group of young adults with learning difficulties, living 'in the community', met with open hostility to the point of stones thrown at their windows:

> I think it's when they get to about nine or ten that the problems really start and I think it's a lot of adult prejudices that are put on to youngsters and they have problems. I think a lot of the public find, I think they still tend to see them not as people in themselves but as people that they want to help but they don't always know the best way of doing that. It's a bit like someone in a wheelchair getting talked about even though they are perfectly capable of answering for themselves, isn't it? But it happens all the way through and I think the more we have kids in mainstream coming into our schools and the more they mix together they are going to grow up with better attitudes and hopefully that should then get through. But in the situation as we are now, yes we do need more of that side of education. But if people aren't willing to interact or get to know people then you still get this business of, 'Oh we're not having them living next door to us', type of thing. All right, we have the problem where I live a while back where they tried to get a small group-home for young men who had been living in

supported accommodation and they wanted them to live a little bit further away because they felt they were capable and would learn from the experience, and they would simply oversee them every so often. The petitions that went around. [They] didn't come to me mind you, but they went all round. A neighbour told me the tale because she said she told them about us. She said, 'What do you think they feel like when you are doing things like this sort of thing?' 'Oh,' she said, 'we wouldn't go to them; we don't mind them living at home with their families,' and I thought, well that says it all really. Those poor young men they didn't have a life because the kids just taunted them, and if they came out and shouted at the kids then it was their fault. But the fact was that the kids had never left them alone, throwing stones at the windows and all this sort of thing, you know?

Post-School Education: Some Tentative Conclusions

There are disproportionately few disabled students in higher education, but it would seem that we need more resources to meet the special and additional needs of disabled students in both the further and higher education sectors. Moreover, students' needs are not always assessed before their courses so that they can be adequately catered for. The problem identified in Chapter 1, of a lack of information about what is available, was found to be a crucial problem in colleges of further and higher education.

Even more inadequate is the provision, in school, of careers advice and preparation for work and the provision of appropriate training, post-school. A much more careful matching of an individual's range of abilities and disabilities would prevent many problems, unsuccessful training placements and unnecessary experiences of failure.

There are at least three good reasons why post-school education, in all its many forms (college courses, evening classes, work-based training, etc.), should improve facilities and support for disabled learners. First, disabled students should have the same opportunities for a lifelong education as other citizens. For there to be real opportunities, some current obstacles and barriers need to be recognised and removed. Second, given that, for various reasons (illness, lack of resources for proper support, lack of intellectual stretching and expectation) many disabled students need and deserve a 'second chance' to acquire various skills and qualifications. Third, the social isolation often associated with unemployment is exacerbated if disabled students also face barriers to leisure-type courses/activities.

Of serious concern is that it is often left to the disabled student to seek the different or additional support or resources that she or he requires. This is time and energy consuming; time and energy needed for study. Moreover, it is often awkward and unpleasant to point out flaws in provision, and some students get labelled as demanding or difficult. It is imperative that the kinds of support and resources that individuals with various kinds of impairment may well require (whether human, such as helpers, or mechanical, such as large print lectures) should be part of the routine provision of mainstream educational institutions.

Unfortunately, the kind of disability awareness on the part of policy makers, heads of departments, finance committees, lecturers and so on that would routinise good practice is largely absent. Hence the need for a much more disability-aware lifelong education for all – school and post-school. Since such disability-aware education is not necessarily built into the personal, social and moral education of children at school, we need to unlearn prejudice in adulthood. And even when mainstream schools do undertake both the inclusion of disabled children and a correlating disability-aware education, it seems that some children will, as adults, still feel ill at ease with disabled adults. Thus formal adult education and, ideally, informal adult education (the media, libraries, theatre) both need to contribute to countering the harmful prejudices, stereotypes and discrimination which are prevalent in society. For disabled citizens are facing such prejudice and discrimination as students and as employees.

CHAPTER 5

Conclusions and Recommendations

This final chapter concludes by setting the previous discussions of the educational experience of disabled people in the current legal and educational framework and then draws out recommendations arising from the particular experiences and views recounted in the 'disability voice' project. It ends by returning to the notion of an enabling education.

The Legal Framework

Relatively recent legislation concerning disabled children and adults has influenced 'special education' and the practice of educational institutions. The Education Act 1993 added to, and in some ways replaced, the arrangements set up by the 1981 Act which incorporated ideas from the Warnock Report (1978) and made legal provisions with wide-reaching 'equal opportunity' implications for children with special educational needs (Leicester 1991); the Education Reform Acts 1986 and 1988 affect all children; and the Disability Discrimination Act 1995 includes requirements for the provision of information from educational institutions.

The Warnock Report, which informed the 1981 Act, had proposed that most pupils currently in special schools should be integrated into ordinary schools; special schools would educate the smaller proportion of pupils with severe or complex disabilities, and should strengthen their links with ordinary schools, offering short-term provision and specialist expertise. They would act as resource centres to help integration become a successful reality. It has to be said that this 'successful reality' has not been fully realised. (Following the Green Paper (1990)the issue of the role of special schools and links between special and ordinary schools are current 'hot issues'.) There seems to be much agreement in special education that adequate resources and funding never matched the requirements or expectations created by the legislation.

In 1990, HMI published a report of their survey into special educational needs. This report was intended for, amongst others, school governors in the 1990s. Entitled *Special Needs Issues*, it reviews progress since Warnock in the light of that report's recommendations. In summary, HMI found that, in many areas of the country, there was a lack of clear statements of policy, of detailed planning in the deployment of personnel and resources, of positive approaches to the management of existing premises and curricula, and of systematic evaluation. They found the most pressing need at all levels for enhanced expertise, particularly in assessing pupils' capabilities in curriculum terms and in providing a broad and balanced curriculum for disabled children. Training had yet to permeate special needs aspects through all subjects taught.

Concerning assessment procedures leading to written statements of special needs, they found considerable variation across LEAs on quality and use of statements and many instances of lack of specificity. However, HMI claimed to find many instances in which statements did succeed in safeguarding children's rights, securing resources and improving monitoring of progress. Overall, they found that the integration of children had proceeded gradually, but that it needed more careful planning, training and resources.

The Education Act 1981 required that children with special educational needs be educated in ordinary schools, subject to the wishes of parents and provided that this was compatible with their receiving the special education they need, with the efficient education of the other children with whom they will be educated, and the efficient use of resources. The LEA had the duty to ensure that special educational provision was made for pupils who needed it. They also had to ensure that, where a pupil was deemed to need it, a statement of their special educational needs was made. The 1993 Act added to the arrangements set up by the 1981 Act and, especially in relation to statementing, replaced it. It provided the Code of Practice discussed in Chapter 3. Teachers, parents, doctors and educational psychologists would be involved in the formal assessment for a statement. The statement must describe the special needs, the special provision required and name the school which would meet those needs. The 1993 Act also set up a new Independent Tribunal to hear parents' appeals against LEA decisions about the special education of their children. In any dispute about school attendance between LEA and parent, the Secretary of State may give a direction. Any such direction to admit a pupil is binding on the governors.

Governors have a duty to ensure that any special provision required by a pupil is provided, that teachers in the school are made aware of the importance of identifying and providing for such pupils, and that the LEA is alerted to the need for a statement. Governors must also appoint a 'responsible person' (e.g. the head or a chair of governors, or another governor), who should be aware of a pupil's special educational needs, which must also be made known to all those likely to teach that child. Governors must also ensure that pupils with statements have the opportunity to engage in activities with children who do not have special needs, provided this is reasonably practicable and that the conditions mentioned previously are able to be met; for example, meeting their special needs and efficient use of resources.

The 1981 and 1993 Acts apply to all pupils with special educational needs. For most pupils with special needs, statementing is not appropriate. Governors and teachers must be concerned with statemented and with this larger and shifting category of non-statemented pupils, though the legislation provides no detailed guidance on how to establish which children should or should not be in each category!

In the provision of these Acts we confront the central dilemma of those educators who are seeking to improve educational provision for disabled pupils and students. The very legislation which at least addresses the educational apartheid and other concerns of disabled people, who are manifestly not receiving equal educational opportunities, does so in a way which enshrines 'disablist' assumptions. (I am using 'disablist' here in a similar way to the more established 'racist' and 'sexist', to mean prejudice/discrimination against disabled people.) It enshrines, that is to say, the notion of 'special need' and of the need to 'statement', and paves the way for complicated and potentially divisive funding arrangements. It is a world away from an educational provision appropriate to student diversity; that is, provision in common schools with differentiation of the curriculum, appropriate teacher training, adequate general levels of resources, and a disability-aware personal and social education for all. Nevertheless, it has brought some improvements within an existing disablist framework and necessarily influences attempts to develop good practice.

The Education Reform Acts 1986 and 1988, though not specifically about special education, do also impact on children with disabilities. The National Curriculum enjoined by the Acts applies to all children, though section 18 provides that for 'statemented children', the requirements may be modified or disapplied for an individual pupil, as specified in the statement. Very few children are disapplied. In addition, the head teacher can temporarily suspend or adapt the National Curriculum for an individual pupil. For example, a child might be 'catching up' in a particular subject after a period of hospitalisation. The head must inform the parents, LEA and governing body, and the parents have the right to appeal to the governing body against the head's decision. Many fear that with the shift of control brought by these Acts, from LEAs to schools, vulnerable groups of children may suffer. For example, Solity (1992) points out that Local Management of Schools, in diverting funds to schools, may have the consequence that funds are not used for the children (with special needs) for whom they were intended. Moreover, LEAs had provided specialist advisors and resources. As schools become more competitive, there is also the concern that if disabled children are perceived to be expensive, or unhelpful in terms of 'league tables', then a place at the mainstream school of one's choice may be more difficult to secure for a disabled child.

The Disability Discrimination Act 1995 introduces, over a period of time, new laws and measures aimed at ending some of the discrimination experienced by many disabled people. The Act gives new rights in employment, access to goods and services, and in relation to buying or renting land or property. The government has produced booklets giving guidance on all aspects of the Act which can be obtained free of charge. The booklets are also available in Braille and on audio cassette (DfEE 1995).

In the educational arena the Act requires schools, colleges and universities to provide information for disabled people. Schools should explain their arrangements for the admission of disabled pupils, how they will help these pupils gain access and what they will do to ensure fair treatment. Further and higher educational institutions should publish statements giving information about facilities for disabled people. LEAs should provide information on their further education facilities for disabled people. While it is possible that these requirements may have, to some extent, improved the information problems that we identified in Chapter 4, it remains the case that there is inadequate and confused communication. Thought needs to be given to how such information is worded and communicated, in consultation with disabled pupils and families and with disabled students and potential students.

What becomes clear from this consideration of the legal framework within which education takes place is that the political and economic climate created by recent educational legislation is not based on a social theory of disability and is both conceptually confused and confusing in practice. It places many demands on schools, but does not match these with appropriate general levels of resource. It may secure some advances within its limitations, though its longer-term effects on the learning and well-being of disabled children seem to be insufficiently monitored. What we must ask ourselves is, 'How can educators work within this legal/economic climate to promote an enabling education for all?' The answer must enjoin working for change at all levels. At school and classroom level, pressure must be exerted and windows of opportunity exploited on behalf of individual disabled pupils and students. At policy level, we need more recognition of institutional discrimination and pressure to change this. At societal level, we can see why disabled people are fighting to end discrimination and to obtain full civil rights. Perhaps the implementation of a much more disability-aware 'education for all' might also help obtain, in the longer term, a more enlightened socio-political/economic framework in which to conduct the important business of 'education, education and education'.

The Educational and Vocational Context

The Swann Report (1985) defined 'institutional discrimination' as the way in which the long-established policies, practices and procedures of an institution (a school or college), which have developed to suit the majority of pupils and students, may discriminate against members of minority groups. Although this definition was offered in the context of the education of minority ethnic groups, the concept is crucial in relation to disability too. Often, when an institution caters for those with the majority range of functions, those with a loss of one of those functions are penalised. They face inappropriate or inadequate procedures. Indeed, the whole notion of a 'special' need is premised on the idea that a minority of people's educational needs do not match those of the majority and therefore constitute additional needs to those which have, simply because they are more widespread, first claim upon educational providers and resources. Examples of institutional discrimination would include: non-provision of key texts in Braille and on tape; printed letters home to blind parents; non-provision of ramps for access to buildings; lack of teacher role models for disabled children; assessment against norms established by reference to an unimpaired group; non-provision of a neighbourhood school for a disabled primary-age child; learning materials full of disablist assumptions and values; and an undifferentiated curriculum designed to suit the 'average' child.

Despite progress in education towards greater inclusion, educational institutions remain bastions of such institutional discrimination. Since prejudiced assumptions underline this discrimination (these biased practices and procedures which are not in the interests of the disabled minority), what has been said about the importance of a disability-aware education is reinforced. However, such an education, in addition to seeking to counter prejudiced attitudes and values, must also equip people to recognise institutional discrimination, which is often subtle and unintentional, and develop their moral will to end it.

Although the barriers created by institutional discrimination are prevalent, as we saw from our respondents, many disabled people succeed educationally despite these hurdles, and live fulfilling and meaningful lives. It is, nevertheless, a matter of justice that such hurdles should be systematically dismantled. Against this general background of institutional discrimination, what *specific* issues are currently important in relation to disabled pupils and students?

Currently, there is an emphasis on increasing standards and much competition between schools. As Geoff Lindsay points out these aims sit uneasily with a service 'for pupils requiring disproportionate support, whose absolute levels of achievement are lower and whose capability for individual responsibility requires longer to develop' (Lindsay 1997, p.29). He argues that when we properly value an education system which emphasises support, collegiality and joint working rather than competition, then we protect children with special educational needs.

Currently, the Education Reform Acts have strengthened a competitive ethos and brought considerable focus on access to the National Curriculum, resourcing, identification and assessment of special needs, assessment of learning, parental involvement and the responsibilities of the school. It is not surprising, then, that some of these issues were aspects of schooling most often discussed by the parents to whom we talked, particularly assessment of special needs, resourcing, integration and parental involvement.

The issue of the assessment of learning, though not directly addressed by the respondents, was implicit in what they had to say about the importance of recognising an individual child's progress and achievements. The Education Reform Acts enjoin assessment at the ends of key stages of schooling. There are nationally prescribed tests and tasks connected with the National Curriculum – referred to as Standard Assessment Tasks. This situation is problematic for children with learning difficulties who do not do themselves justice in terms of their learning achievements on standard tests. Solity (1992) points out that the principal educational aim of assessment should be to find out whether children are progressing in their learning, and since they learn at differing rates from varying starting points, it is arguable that comparing a child's performance with a norm is not particularly useful, and that criterion-referenced assessment, which seeks to discover what children have or have not learned in specific areas of the Curriculum, gives little information about how they learned or failed to learn. Solity outlines an approach to assessment known as 'assessment through teaching', widely advocated in the field of special needs because it provides information about how to facilitate a given child's progress. This seems to match the parents' insistence that their child's progress be measured in terms of his or her individual progress within a learning environment geared to his or her specific learning needs.

Post-school, we find an educational context which emphasises the acquisition of competencies through the collection of National Vocational Qualifications (NVQs) or their equivalent. As Tomlinson and Coloquhoun (1993) have pointed out, the implication is that if young people are not employable it is because they have not gained such skills and qualifications, and not that there is anything wrong with the economic structures. Young people with 'special educational needs' are likely to find more difficulty in collecting NVQs and so on, and Tomlinson and Coloquhoun argue that in the restructured vocational education and training systems of the 1990s, those with special educational needs are likely to have less NVQs and thus be 'reinforced in their lowly position in a low wage workforce'. However, they point out that availability of work rests on such factors as 'national and global investment, the retention of manufacturing industry, the expansion of public sector employment and planned employment policies'. They also point out that a more adequate symbiosis between competition and collaboration would enable more inclusive employment policies to be developed. They conclude: 'However, in the UK, the signs are that a model of exclusion with the "specials" in their familiar place as a special (un)employable underclass, defined largely as "deficients" or "less competent" will predominate' (Tomlinson and Coloquhoun 1993, p.87).

This very important argument should be re-emphasised in the current debates about moving people from 'Welfare to Work'. Training and incentives can only lead to work for the unemployed, including the disabled unemployed, in so far as there are genuine employment prospects – real jobs for all.

Recommendations for Good Practice

There are many recommendations one could make, of varying degrees of generality and at all levels of the system, to encourage good practice in school and post-school educational provision. Since one strategy for securing progressive change is to share such good practice as does exist and to disseminate ideas about it, I have reproduced, as Appendix 1, features of good practice which were identified in an OECD review (OECD 1995) of established integration programmes. These could certainly be read as a wide-ranging list of recommendations covering educational organisation, curriculum, parental and community involvement, support services, training and resourcing.

Less ambitiously, in this section I draw out such recommendations for practice as seem to be implied by the experiences and views of our 'disability voice' respondents. It is worth noting here that a more recent and very similar piece of research to the 'disability voice' project produced very similar findings. Pilgrim conducted 26 interviews of adults with acquired physical impairments (Pilgrim 1997). As in our project, these researchers used an open-ended interview schedule and conducted interviews of between one and two hours' duration, making contacts through a range of networks. Shared and crucial findings include a professional lack of efficiency at communicating existing entitlement arrangements; discriminatory experience in employment; and lack of access in the social environment, including transport problems (getting on and off buses, for example). The good practice they endorsed also matches several of the recommendations to be made in this section, including the importance of good interpersonal skills for health and welfare professionals and efficient advice about entitlements. The researchers conclude by emphasising the importance of the views of disabled people to the improvement of the service and of political activism of service commissioners alongside disabled people.

In making the recommendations that follow I am not suggesting that some schools and colleges are not already in engaged in good practice. Nevertheless, since there is evidence of great variability in practice and provision, it is likely that many institutions still have 'a long way to go'.

Professional Training: Health and Welfare Professionals

In Chapter 2 we saw how important and significant had been the process of diagnosis of impairment in the lives of our respondents. At this time of crisis we saw the importance of improving communication between the individual and the medical/health care professionals involved. This clearly has implications for their professional education and training. Such education and training should include disability awareness. It should also incorporate more vocationally specific learning, including communication skills for doctors and knowledge of the relevant range of welfare benefits and information services for all professionals working with disabled people.

Professional Training: Teachers., Lecturers and Other Education Staff

There is a 'continuum of training' about 'special needs' for teachers, with some introduction for all teachers during initial training, followed up by in-service training, particularly for those involved in integration programmes, with additional training for specialist teachers and SENCOs.

(Cowne 1996). There is no such systematic 'continuum' for teachers of adults. Given the prevalence of negative attitudes and disablist assumptions encountered by many disabled people, it is clearly important that all training incorporates an 'equal opportunity' dimension. In other words, teachers, lecturers and other educational staff should receive a training which includes disability awareness as well as 'special needs' skills. Such education/training should provide a curriculum which would develop a greater awareness of disablist prejudice and discrimination as well as vocationally specific learning, such as teaching techniques relevant to specific kinds of impairment.

A 'talk and chalk' approach may not facilitate attitudinal change. With more emphasis on inclusion, disabled people being their own best advocates, a 'radical pedagogy' would allow students to learn from each other and from their individual experiences of oppression (Giroux 1992), and experiential exercises may facilitate emotional engagement, self-knowledge and a process of attitudinal awareness and change. Such experiential teaching approaches, including role play, dialogue, structured discussions, workshops and 'games' and tasks, have been used in a variety of prejudice reduction and awareness programmes (e.g. Katz 1978; Sears and Williams 1998).

Since in mainstream schools all teachers are responsible for meeting the (special) educational needs of pupils, there is a general recognition of the importance of a 'whole-school' approach. It is likely, therefore, that more whole-school in-service training would be fruitful. Again this should include a disability-aware perspective.

Nor must governors be neglected. LEAs and schools should provide training for governors in order to support them in undertaking their 'special needs' responsibilities within a 'disability-aware' perspective. (In the governor training provision following the Education Reform Acts, we found relatively little 'equal opportunity' training on offer and even less taken up (Leicester and Lovell 1994b).)

Our respondents emphasised the uniqueness of impaired individuals and the diversity of individual needs. This endorses the importance of a differentiated curriculum. Since within-class curriculum differentiation demands high levels of skill among class teachers, this too carries strong implications for teacher training. (There is evidence of a lack of effective monitoring of teacher training programmes (OECD 1995).)

Resources

Two key issues emerged from our interview data: the prevalence of negative public attitudes to disabled people and the inadequacy of resources. The issue of negative attitudes has influenced the foregoing emphasis on the importance of health/welfare/education professional education and training. It is because of negative attitudes and assumptions that it is so important that such training includes disability issues and a disability-aware perspective to counter disablist approaches. What similarly important implications, then, can be drawn in relation to that second emerging key issue – the inadequacy of all kinds of resources? (It is perhaps worth noting that our respondents' experience of inadequate resourcing is supported by head teachers, who are concerned that general cuts in LEA budgets are adversely affecting pupils with special needs.) Our parent respondents felt that there should be more resources to meet the special needs identified in their children's statements. (There does seem, also, to be a pressing need for LEAs to clarify how resources for special needs are allocated to schools and how they are used to support pupils, and for resource allocation for statemented and non-statemented children not to be in competition.) Leaving aside the confusing complexity of resource structures, it must be said that the levels of support for disabled pupils seem to be inadequate – even relative to a general inadequacy in educational funding.

The other clearly emerging resource issue was that of inadequate information. Lack of information about benefits and other resources adversely affected our respondents, and such information should surely be more routinely built into a whole variety of social practices. In education, as in the welfare field, this seems an arena where improvements could be made. Direct communication with parents would help them to be clearer about procedures such as the periodic review of statementing.

College students also complained of inadequate information. Through it is now mandatory that colleges ensure that existing special resources and support networks are made known to disabled students before and upon starting their courses, there are failures in this which suggest more monitoring of the processes involved may be required.

Physical access provided by the campus (lifts, toilets, ramps, car park facilities, etc.) should be monitored and continue to be systematically improved.

The views and experiences of disabled students at the institution should be sought in this process.

On a more specific note, a visually impaired student pointed out that large-print notes of lectures and seminars, in advance of the lecture and seminar, would be useful.

Schooling

In Chapter 3 we considered the experience of schooling. Issues about special schools, about statementing and about integration emerged, and suggest the following recommendations.

Bearing in mind that children do not fit neatly into our categorisation of 'special schools', it was felt important that child, parents and professionals together seek to select the most appropriate school.

Parents emphasised that special schools should make special efforts to involve parents in the life of the school, consult them and be supportive to the family.

Teachers should seek to stretch pupils academically and recognise achievement – measured in terms of an individual child's efforts and progress and not against an age-referenced 'norm'.

One disabled adult respondent recommended that logo/labelling on special school transport be avoided.

Parents highlighted that those involved in the statementing process should be reminded of the danger of labels and be encouraged to capture the unique and specific combination of needs for each child. Schools which draw up and make use of good individual educational plans may be in a better position to identify and record needs with greater specificity.

Our respondents had much to say in relation to the issue of 'integration'. There was substantial support for the view that many of the children traditionally educated in separate special schools could and should benefit from mainstream provision. However, it was felt that this inclusion must go hand in hand with more disability awareness in mainstream pupils and teachers and adequate levels of resources. (Internationally, inclusion has worked best where there are financial systems in place for ensuring that the process is fully funded through policy which has redirected funds from segregation to inclusive provision (see Thomas *et al.* 1998).)

Link projects were found to be a potentially useful way of providing inclusion for disabled children. Such schemes should, with proper preparation and monitoring, continue to be encouraged and increased. Links with local special schools could also be used to draw on the expertise of special school staff in training and support for mainstream teachers.

As stated in the Code of Practice, when a child transfers to a mainstream school SENCOs could set up regular meetings with the parents to discuss ways in which they could help their child with home and class work. Our parent respondents' concern for their children's education and for their future suggests that many parents would welcome such involvement. The parent respondents also talked about their children's out-of-school activities since these contribute to a child's learning and well-being at the schooling stage. They thought that more attention should be given to 'special needs' provision outside school. For example, one parent recommended that children's playgrounds and play areas, in public parks and elsewhere, should cater for children with a range of impairments, and several mentioned difficulties with public transport.

Education Beyond School

In Chapter 4 we considered post-school education – in further and higher education, in careers advice and training, and in terms of any informal 'education for all'. Our disabled adult respondents, in particular, suggested many improvements that could be made to this education beyond school. They suggested that disabled young people, in the transition from school to further education, should be fully involved in discussions and decisions about, their future. Students with learning impairment are entitled to be treated as adults with as full a responsibility for decisions about their own lives and time as possible. It was recommended that a student's needs be fully assessed before he or she begins his or her study so that learning is not impeded.

It was strongly felt by several respondents that not only should colleges continue to use consultative structures and nominate staff who will monitor the needs and progress of disabled students, but that colleges should seek to ensure that students are not expected to take the initiative, without the support of institutional structures, in drawing unmet special needs to institutional attention.

We also learned from our disabled adult respondents that careers advice and training had been inadequate. However, as a result of the Code of Practice LEAs must now invite the careers service to all annual reviews of children with special needs after their fourteenth birthday. This emphasis on transition planning may have improved the quality of careers advice and preparation compared with that experienced by our respondents. There is also some evidence that employment schemes in local businesses which use co-workers to support a person with learning disabilities 'on the job' have been much more successful than the traditional vocational training centres in generating paid, productive work (Tackney 1992).

Drawing on their particular experience, 'careers' recommendations emerging from our respondents included the following:

- Youth training schemes should be improved in relation to the needs of disabled students.

- Careful consideration of each individual's range of abilities and disabilities (possibly through detailed portfolios) should precede training placements.

- Employment interviews should follow good equal opportunity guidelines to avoid discrimination through unwarranted questions and biased assumptions.

- The trainer and the employer should take responsibility, devising appropriate structures, for monitoring provision and support for disabled employees.

- Flexible working conditions (e.g. flexi-time) and the provision of restrooms would be helpful for many (disabled and able-bodied) employees.

- Given that disabled adults often fail to achieve their educational potential, 'second chance' educational opportunities in 'adult education' are important and should be assessed and considerably developed in relation to students with special needs.

- Local authorities should, in view of the disproportionate number of unemployed disabled people, ensure that accessible leisure provision is available.

Last, we turn to the issue of informal education. The 'disability voice' interviews strongly suggest the need for a public better informed and better educated about disability. Unfortunately, there is little evidence that the mass media are making much of a contribution to such an endeavour. Indeed, charitable advertising and television programmes about the 'plight' of disabled people may reinforce stereotypes, encourage pathologising perspectives and generate a patronising pity. We need, therefore, much more positive attempts at incorporating positive images in the media combined with systematic disability-aware (experiential) education in schools and colleges.

McConkey (1995) points out that the consensus from research on changing attitudes towards disabled people is that enjoyable interaction with a peer who is 'handicapped' invariably produces positive changes. Researchers have found that it is the quality rather than the quantity of interaction which is important. These findings would support what we have said about link schemes for schools. They also support the importance of the 'informal learning' generated when disabled children and adults are included in community life.

Within formal post-school education, as for school education, all courses, from liberal leisure provision to vocational training, should be permeated with disability awareness, with more courses or components of courses specifically about equal opportunities for disabled people. Unfortunately, there is less systematic pre- and in-service training for lecturers in colleges and universities than for teachers in schools. There is, therefore, a real problem about who will 'train the trainers' for this disability-aware provision.

Towards an Enabling Education

It seems clear that if we want a reorientation of currently prejudiced social attitudes towards disability, and if we want to provide equal opportunities for disabled people, then we must promote and achieve substantial educational change. Only radical reorganisation will achieve the (successful) inclusion of disabled children into mainstream education. In the meantime, a hundred-and-one smaller changes could at least improve their educational experiences.

Of course, in seeking to improve practice we must move from a particular starting place and context. Since that starting place and context is one of oppressive structures and attitudes, realistic decisions and judgements are often not about radical change but about incremental gains towards an ideal. For example, inadequate resources will sometimes mean working out the least poor provision in the circumstances. Moreover, non-ideal and complex situations of oppression often present individuals with very real dilemmas. Think, for instance, of parents who believe strongly in the principle of integration and who would like their child to be educated alongside siblings and local neighbourhood friends or potential friends, and yet who have good reason to fear that their child would be hurt in an unchanged mainstream school, in various ways. Similarly, several of our parent respondents mentioned inadequate provision of one-to-one tuition. Yet, as Solity (1992) has pointed out, children derive considerable benefit from working collaboratively alongside their peers and in so doing learn many important social skills. But given an actual situation such that appropriate group work is not provided, it is small wonder that parents want one-to-one teacher time. Again, the choice is not between such tuition and an ideal learning environment, but between such tuition and the experience of being in a class where an undifferentiated curriculum is proving inaccessible. (Ideally teachers need more time for preparation and planning of whole-class work.) Or think of the dilemma of the head teacher or teacher who simply does not have the resources to meet the needs identified in a child's statement. It is not surprising that changes such as those discussed in this chapter will often be a struggle and have a political dimension.

Nevertheless, we must strive for good practice in both school and the post-school sectors. This should include attention to a disability-aware education for all students as well as to adequate and flexible provision to meet so-called 'special needs'. Disability awareness education will not only seek prejudice reduction and attitudinal change, but the development of skills to identify discriminatory structures and commitment to devise more progressive ones. Education to meet special needs must be a lifelong matter since impairment or deterioration of a condition can occur at any stage of the life-span, bringing new educational needs. Given an ageing population, an increasingly high proportion of us will experience our own disability – education could better prepare us for this, not least in terms of escaping a legacy of social prejudice likely to damage our own self-esteem.

Until a radical reorientation in socio-political thinking transcends the notion of 'special needs', in practical terms all this means changes in the role and functioning of special schools, with better links between special and mainstream sectors and increased resources for special needs provision in special and mainstream schools. It also implies the need for curriculum differentiation to increase access to the curriculum for disabled people, curriculum development and to encourage in all pupils the unlearning of prejudice, and the acquisition of skills to identify institutional discrimination.

In institutions of further and higher education, we have seen the need for better information and support systems and for more effective careers advice and training. All adult education, from liberal leisure courses to vocational updating, could be more disability-aware. Moreover, it has been suggested that the informal education provided by the media, by libraries and recreational services should have regard to what is called the 'education for all' dimension. In this way, we conceive of an enabling education within a framework of lifelong learning.

There is currently much discussion about the development of the 'learning society'. A widespread recognition and reorientation of negative attitudes to, and unfair discrimination against, the disabled should be an intrinsic part of this vision.

The Three Rs: Rights, Respect and Resources

I have talked of a 'reorientation' of attitudes towards disability. In effect this is to move away from a perspective that locates disability with the individual and blames and devalues individuals with certain sorts of impairment. Within this perspective, even humane people tend to exhibit a kindly patronisation, rather than automatically to recognise the full civil rights of every person. In a reasonably prosperous and civilised society, whatever our range of abilities and disabilities, each of us should surely have an equal right to an education which stretches us academically, and which is also vocationally useful, within a framework of adequate pastoral care. (One might add, here, that one mark of a civilised society is how well it treats its most vulnerable citizens.) Thus we will no longer think in terms of special provision for those who deviate from some norm constructed in relation to an average ability range or a majority set of skills. Rather, we will think in terms of each individual's learning styles and requirements, with correspondingly more differentiation within the curriculum.

This emphasis on rights goes hand in hand with respect – respect for each individual as a unique centre of consciousness and a full citizen; such respect seems not to be encouraged in a culture of conformity which devalues legitimate differences between individuals.

Going further along the road towards such an enabling education does not necessarily cost more. For example, research has indicated that it costs society more to educate a child in a special school than properly supported in the mainstream:

> While comparative costs of integrated and segregated education are extremely difficult to estimate, such evidence as there is points consistently in the same direction. It appears that, for the majority of children with special needs, education in integrated settings is not inordinately costly and in any case less expensive than their placement in special schools. Integration can be helped or hindered by methods of allocating funding. For example, funding to ordinary schools can be linked to integration programmes, can include realistic additional elements to allow for the extra costs of education of children with special needs, and can be sensitive to different levels of special need. (Hegarty 1995)

However, if some additional provision *is* required for the effective learning of an individual, let her claim on collective resources be recognised within a framework of respect for individuality and for the rights of each individual.

Sadly, even as I come to the end of these reflections, the present Labour government is said to be contemplating cuts to disability benefits. As we have clearly seen in sharing the experiences of our respondents, more, not fewer, resources are needed for social and educational sufficiency. Like me, many citizens feel angry and hurt that our government can think this 'unthinkable'. Can we really contemplate taking money from those living on benefits alone? Of course, the government would do well to improve the employment prospects of the disabled, but this would be better done by more effective enforcement of the quota system and by better resourced support for those in employment than by cutting the benefits of the disabled unwaged. And for those with a salary, why should a benefit which recognises the financial costs which impairments bring be means tested?

I should add that in a reply from 10 Downing Street, to a letter of concern I had written about this, I have been assured that there has been no decision to cut benefits for the disabled and the sick (and this has, so far, held good). Indeed, I am told that tackling social exclusion and providing equal opportunities and empowering disabled people to play a full role in society is a key priority of the government. There is a promise to tackle discrimination against disabled people. This letter (which is reproduced as Appendix 2) ends with this sentence: 'The current system is not working for disabled people and we need to modernise it.'

Time will tell whether central government decisions will take a step away or a step towards enablement and equality for disabled people. In the meantime, as educational professionals, we must continue to attempt to develop better practice in relation to all our pupils' educational needs.

OECD Report by the Centre for Research Innovation into the Integration of Students with Special Needs Into Mainstream Schools

Features of Good Practice
Educational Organisation

- government, regional and district education policies state that, wherever practicable, children with special educational needs should be educated in ordinary classes in ordinary schools – school policies endorse and actively promote this principle

- policy makers at all levels, including school level, regularly reaffirm their commitment to integration and take opportunities, for example by publicising successful examples, to promote and sustain positive attitudes, among children, among teachers and among other adults in the community, towards those with special needs

- government, regional and district education authorities monitor, evaluate and actively review the implementation of their integration policies

- district education authorities ensure that children with special needs have access to educational opportunities in integrated settings well before they reach statutory school age

- a main agreed objective of the schools in a district is together to provide effective education for all the children in that district

- within ordinary schools, children do not have to repeat a year in order to reach a certain standard before moving up into the next year group

- schools continuously assess the progress of their children with special educational needs and periodically review their provision – assessment is of social adjustment as well as of academic achievement and may lead to social training programmes, perhaps aimed at reducing social isolation and low self-esteem

- where special schools are shifting from direct provision for children to the provision of advisory and training services to ordinary schools, they maintain a balance of staffing to ensure that both kinds of provision continue to be effective

- transition of children from special schools to ordinary schools sometimes involves considerable preparation, which may include briefing
  special school children on the ways of ordinary schools, providing opportunities for ordinary school and special school class teachers to see
  one another at work as well as to discuss the children, and running
  sessions with teachers, children and parents in ordinary schools to
  help them understand and develop positive attitudes towards children
  with special needs
- when children with special educational needs require extra education
  support to follow the ordinary school curriculum, this normally occurs
  within ordinary classrooms rather than through small-group with-
  drawal or placement in special classes
- time allocated to class teachers and support teachers enables them to
  consult, assess and plan as well as to teach
- schools have resource bases designed to support and enhance the provision of special education within the ordinary curriculum.

Curriculum

- school accommodation is designed to ensure that children with sensor
  and motor disabilities have the same access to schools as do other
  children of the same age; this involves not only access to the different
  areas of the schools but also access to their learning opportunities
- curriculum planning at school level implements a whole-school policy
  for special needs and ensures a balanced curriculum for all
- where schools implement a common curriculum at each age level, this
  is modified to meet the differing needs of children of differing abilities
- where schools run different curriculum options for different children,
  they are presented as being appropriate to children's differing abilities
  and interests but not as hierarchies in which some are intrinsically
  superior to others
- where a child with special needs is being introduced to an ordinary
  class from a special school or special class, integration by easy stages
  may be appropriate, for example, by starting with practical rather than
  academic subjects
- within each class, the teacher uses a range of strategies to take account
  of differing abilities – for example, allowing children to complete the
  same work at different rates, allowing some children to complete work
  in simplified form, and from time to time setting different group or individual work for different children

- for children with special needs there is a continuum of support, ranging from minimal help in ordinary classrooms to increasingly specialised learning programmes and increasing advice and support from specialist teachers and external support service staff
- occasionally children with special needs are withdrawn from ordinary classes particular types of work, for example, for sign language training or for physiotherapy – when this happens, the class teacher ensures that this does not unduly upset the balance of their curriculum or cause them to miss out on any vital element
- class teachers and support teachers work together flexibly, exchanging roles on occasion, together ensuring that all the children in the classes, not just those with special needs, progress optimally.

Parental and Community Involvement

- at all stages of national developments in integration, representatives of parent organisations are involved on a consultative basis
- as district and within-school integration programmes are developed, parents of children with special needs, along with representatives of the communities more generally, are consulted from the outset of each stage and are invited to participate
- when parents of children with special educational needs seek to initiate or further develop integration programmes, their views are taken as seriously by decision makers as are those of professionals
- parents are treated as partners in assessment, decision making and review when their children are being considered by staff of schools and external support services with a view to special educational provision
- parents of children with special educational needs are represented on the governing bodies of schools
- where appropriate, parents and other members of the community are encouraged to be present in classrooms and to share in the work of the schools
- parents of children with special needs, particularly parents of preschool children, are helped by professionals to develop the skills needed to teach their own children.

Support Services

- district education authorities ensure that the progress of children with significant disabilities is monitored and that their provision is reviewed periodically

- where formal assessment of children's special needs is undertaken, this involves consultation with parents and draws on appropriate specialisms but does not cause inordinate delay in securing appropriate provision

- staff of external support services apply and develop their advisory and in-service training skills, particularly in relation to within-school support staff, rather than focusing largely on assessment and placement

- staff of support services negotiate specific and finite arrangements, including learning targets, for the support they are to provide

- staff of support services, in consultation with school staff and parents, plan and monitor the transition of students with special needs from schools to suitable post-school experience

- staff of external support services and outreach staff of special schools confer to ensure that their services are complementary and together meet local needs.

Training

- initial teacher training courses ensure that all trainees gain awareness of special needs, some knowledge of disabilities and some skills in teaching children of varying abilities in normal classes

- initial teacher training courses provide options enabling trainees with particular interests and aptitudes in special education to develop further knowledge and skills

- teacher training establishments meet the needs for training to higher degree level in all major aspects of special education, including training to apply the expertise gained in fulfilling researching, innovating, inspectorial, administrative, managerial, advisory and teacher training roles

- staff of teacher training establishments confer regularly with external support service staff and other providers of professional development in special education, to ensure that their respective contributions within their regions are complementary and together amount to comprehensive provision

- regional and district education authorities monitor provision of in-service training arrangements in special education, to ensure that the needs of all their schools are met effectively

- all teachers have professional development opportunities sufficient to enable them to understand and teach the children with special needs in their classes

- schools run induction programmes designed to ensure that newly appointed staff are aware of school policy and practice concerning children with special needs, and become familiar with any particular methods, teaching materials and equipment used
- where appropriate, special education in-service training opportunities for teachers are also made open to other school staff and to parents
- where needed, school and external support service staff help parents develop advocacy skills, including those of negotiation
- ordinary school support staff concerned with special needs have access to the training required to enable them to develop the teaching, evaluation, advisory, training and problem-solving skills they need
- special school staff undertaking outreach work have the in-service training opportunities required to develop the range of skills needed for support work in ordinary schools.

Resourcing

- government education departments ensure that the supply of teachers and arrangements for their training are sufficient to enable national integration policies to be fully implemented
- at national level, distribution of educational resources does not encourage regional and district authorities to place children with special needs in special schools rather than in ordinary schools
- the distribution of resources to schools takes realistic account of the differences in expenditure required to provide appropriate education for children of differing abilities, and in doing so builds in some incentives for teachers in ordinary schools to provide for children with special needs in ordinary classes
- resourcing of integration programmes allows for their being relatively costly at initiation and during the earlier stages of their implementation, and takes realistic account of the costs of continued monitoring once they are established – evaluation is built into the programmes from the start
- within schools, banks of teaching materials and associated technical equipment are developed and maintained, to enable class teachers to differentiate their work to cater for children of differing abilities and to ensure that children with sensory or motor disabilities have full access to the curriculum – some of these resources may be developed and stored on an across-schools basis.

Letter of Reply Received January 1998
from 10 Downing Street

1O DOWNING STREET
LONDON SW1A 2AA

From the Political Office   8th January 1998

Dear Mr Leicester

The Prime Minister has asked me to thank you for your letter.

I can assure you that there has been no decision to cut benefits for the disabled and the sick. Disabled people who are in genuine need of benefit will not lose out. Reforming the Welfare State to tackle social exclusion and welfare dependency is a key priority of the Government. We want to give sick and disabled people the same opportunities enjoyed by other people, and empower them to play a full role in society. The Labour Government of 1945 built the Welfare State. The Labour approach is to modernise the Welfare State around the 1945 principles of opportunity and fairness by promoting work for those who can work and a better and fairer deal for those who cannot.

Many disabled people and people with health problems want to work. That is why, in the Budget, we announced our *New Deal for the Long-Term Sick and Disabled*, which will use £195 million from the windfall tax, to develop a package of measures to provide opportunities to work for people with disabilities and health problems.

Our Comprehensive Spending Review of benefits paid to sick and disabled people and their carers will make sure that the social security system assists people to work and achieve economic independence where they want it and provides effective support to those sick and disabled people who are unlikely ever to be able to work to enable them to live independently and with dignity.

We will also tackle discrimination against disabled people by taking action on civil rights and establishing a Disability Rights Commission.

We were elected on a platform of change to build a modern Britain. We were elected to govern for all the people. Disabled people must be able to play their full part, free from old barriers and prejudice. The current system is not working for disabled people and we need to modernise it.

Yours sincerely

Caroline Adams

References

Abberley, P. (1987) 'The concept of oppression and the development of a social theory of disability.' *Disability, Handicap and Society 2*, 1, 5–19.

Allport, W.H. (1958) *Prejudice*. New York: Doubleday.

Baier, C. (1987) 'The need for more than justice.' *Canadian Journal of Philosophy*.

Cowne, E. (1996) *The SENCO Handbook. Working Within a Whole School Approach*. London: David Fulton Publishers.

Derrington, C., Evans, C. and Lee, B. *(1996) The Code in Practice. The Impact on Schools and LEAs*. Slough: NFER.

Department for Education and Employment (1995) *Disability Discrimination*. Circular 3/97. PPY341 (Braille); PPY342 (Audio). London: DfEE.

Friedman, M. (1987) 'Beyond caring: the de-moralization of gender.' *Canadian Journal of Philosophy*. Supplement 13.

Gilligan, C. (1982) *In A Different Voice*. Cambridge, MA: Harvard University Press.

Giroux, H. (1992) *Border Crossings*. London: Routledge.

Griffin, C. (1987) *Accessing Prior Learning: Progress and Practice*. London: Learning From Experience Trust.

Hall, J. (1997) *Social Devaluation and Special Education: The Right to Full Mainstream Education and an Honest Statement*. London: Jessica Kingsley Publishers.

Hasler (1993) 'Development in the disabled people's movement.' In J. Swain *et al.* (eds) *Disabling Barriers – Enabling Education*. Buckingham: Sage, OUP.

Hegarty, S. (1989) 'Post, current and future research or integration.' In N. Jones (ed) *Special Educational Needs Review*. Brighton: Falmer Press.

Hegarty, S. (1995) 'Resources.' In *Integrating Students with Special Needs into Mainstream Schools*. Paris: OECD.

Hepburn, E.R. (1994) 'Women and ethics: a seeing justice?' *Journal of Moral Education 23*, 1, 27–38.

Katz, J. (1978) *White Awareness: A Handbook for Anti-Racism Training*. Oklahoma City: University of Oklahoma Press.

Kohlberg, L. (1981) *The Philosophy of Moral Development*. London: Harper & Row.

Lee, B. and Henkhuzens, Z. (1996) *Integration in Progress: Pupils with Special Needs in Mainstream Schools.* Slough: NFER.

Leicester, M. (1989) *Multicultural Education: From Theory to Practice.* Windsor: NFER-Nelson.

Leicester, M. (1991) *Equal Opportunities in School.* London: Longman.

Leicester, M. (1993) *Race for a Change in Continuing and Higher Education.* Buckingham: OUP.

Leicester, M. (1994) 'Special children, integration and moral education.' *Children and Society 8,* 4, 300–312.

Leicester, M. (ed) (1996) 'Equal opportunities in education: a coherent, rational and moral concern.' *Journal of Philosophy of Education 30,* 2, 207–225.

Leicester, M. and Lovell, T. (1992) 'Comment.' *Studies in the Education of Adults 24,* 1, 7–9.

Leicester, M. and Lovell, T. (1994) 'Equal opportunity training for governors as adult education.' *Studies in the Education of Adults, September* 50–67.

Leicester, M. and Lovell, T. (1994a) 'Race, gender and disability; a comparative perspective.' *Journal of Further and Higher Education Spring* 52–56.

Lewis, A. (1995) *Children's Understanding of Disability.* London: Routledge.

Lindsay, G. (1997) 'Values, rights and dilemmas.' *British Journal of Special Education 24,* 2.

McConkey, R. (1995) 'Seen through a glass darkly: modifying public attitudes.' In P. Mitler and V. Sinason (eds) *Changing Policy and Practice for People with Learning Disabilities.* London: Cassell.

Millet, S. (1987) Only correct: the place of self-knowledge in ethics.

Mittler, P. and Sinason, V. (1996) *Changing Policy and Practice for People with Learning Disabilities.* London: Cassell.

OECD (1995) *Integrating Students with Special Needs into Mainstream Schools.* Paris: OECD.

Priestley, M. (1998) 'Constitutions and creations: idealism, materialism and disability theory.' *Disability and Society 13,* 1, 75–95.

Rawls, J. (1971) *A Theory of Justice.* Cambridge, MA: Harvard University Press.

Samad, K. and Fairbairn, S. (1992) 'Equal opportunities and integration – a mainstream perspective.' In G. Fairbairn and S. Fairbairn (eds) *Integrating Special Children: Some Ethical Issues.* Aldershot: Avebury.

Schön, D.A. (1983) *The Reflective Practitioner: How Professionals Think in Action.* New York: Basic Books.

Sears, J. And Williams, W. (1998) *Overcoming Heterosexism and Homophobia: Strategies that Work.* New York: Columbia University Press.

Shearer, A. (1981) *Disability: Whose Handicap?* Oxford: Basil Blackwell.

Solity, J. (1992) *Special Education*. London: Cassell.

Special Issue: Narrative and Autobiography (1991) *Journal of Moral Education* 20, 3.

Special Issue: Auto/Biography in Sociology. (1993) *Journal of British Sociological Association* 27, 1.

Swain, J. *et al.* (eds) (1993) *Disabling Barriers – Enabling Environments*. Buckingham: Sage/OUP.

Swann Report (1985) *Education for All*. London: HMSO.

Thomas, G., Walker, D. and Webb, J. (1998) *The Making of the Inclusive School*. London: Routledge.

Tomlinson, S. and Coloquhoun, R.F. (1993) 'The political economy of special education needs in Britain.' *Disability and Society 10*, 2.

Warnock, M. (1978) *Report of the Committee of Enquiry into the Education of Handicapped Children and Young People*. London: HMSO.

Wittgenstein, L. (1953) *Philosophical Investigations*. Oxford: Basil Blackwell.

Subject Index